Influence Starts with "I"

With our compliments

THE INSTITUTE FOR MANAGEMENT STUDIES

Delivering Excellence in
Executive Education Since 1974

(775) 322-8222
IMS-online.com

Influence Starts with "I"

A Woman's Guide for Unleashing the Power of Leading
from Within and Effecting Change Around You

Jeanne Porter King

FOREWORD BY
Debbye Turner Bell

RESOURCE *Publications* · Eugene, Oregon

INFLUENCE STARTS WITH "I"
A Woman's Guide for Unleashing the Power of Leading from Within and
Effecting Change Around You

Resource Publications
An Imprint of Wipf and Stock Publishers
199 W. 8th Ave., Suite 3
Eugene, OR 97401

www.wipfandstock.com

PAPERBACK ISBN: 978-1-5326-6294-2
HARDCOVER ISBN: 978-1-5326-6295-9
EBOOK ISBN: 978-1-5326-6296-6

Cover Image Source: Shutterstock, AlexXML

Manufactured in the U.S.A.

To the memories of Dr. Chandra Taylor Smith and Dr. Charleyse Pratt: You both were my sister-colleagues who led from within and brought about tremendous change around you. The world lost you both way too soon, but your influence lives on.

Contents

Foreword

Dr. Jeanne Porter King is a force of nature. When I met her many years ago, we instantly bonded. We were both facilitators at a women's conference. At the time I thought that bond was born out of our common backgrounds, values, and stations in life. Over time, I began to realize that Jeanne is the kind of dynamic person that makes those with whom she interacts feel empowered, special, and uplifted. Her keen intelligence, vast knowledge of women in leadership, and broad experience in coaching, mentoring, and training women leaders inspires and challenges women to be the best version of their true selves. She is the embodiment of excellence, confidence, and influence. Plainly stated, Jeanne's principles on leadership and influence are extensions of her own character.

I have experienced first-hand the positive response Jeanne's teaching on influence elicits. Her approach to equipping women leaders with tools for success is rooted in impeccable research, organized in easily understood concepts, and delivered with power and warmth. Common reactions to Jeanne's teaching on influence are "I never thought of influence in this way," "I am so excited to put these principles into practice," and "This is one of the best workshops I've ever taken!" Now, Jeanne has put that powerful teaching into this book, *Influence Starts with "I."* And value is added because *Influence Starts with "I"* synthesizes more than twenty years of training, coaching, mentoring, and leading.

These are exciting times to be a woman. Women are being heard like never before in business, politics, and community. Women have cracked, if not broken through, glass ceilings as CEOs, entrepreneurs, change agents, and activists. While women are achieving new heights personally and professionally, we are facing challenges as leaders and emerging leaders that are unique to womanhood. As women strive for work-life balance, professional advancement, and personal fulfillment, it is imperative to fully appreciate the power of our purpose, individuality, and passion. And that's where *Influence Starts with "I"* provides invaluable insight and instruction.

The real power of this book lies in giving yourself fully to the process. Don't just read to glean information. Be open to true (and sometimes difficult) self-reflection. Take the time to answer the reflection/discussion questions that Jeanne poses at the end of each chapter. Your answers to these questions will help the lessons therein bloom beyond the words on the pages. Also, every chapter comes with an opportunity to act on the principles. These "action" items animate the lesson and help you get a "3-D" understanding of the practical application of the chapter's insights.

Influence Starts with "I" is part manifesto, part inspiration, part instruction manual, and part masterclass. For women (and men who want to understand and support women) who want to realize the full potential of their true purpose and talents, this book is required reading. Essential elements of success for women in life and work include vision, confidence, communication, and initiative. All of these qualities require a full understanding of influence. *Influence Starts with "I"* will shepherd the reader through grasping the importance of influence, identifying your individual strengths and purpose, developing influence strategies, negotiating barriers, and creating a plan of action to bring influence to life in your career, community, family, and friendships.

Dr. Debbye Turner Bell

CEO and Founder, Debbye Turner Bell Consulting
Veterinarian/Trainer/Motivational Speaker/Broadcast Journalist
Miss America 1990

Introduction

I alone cannot change the world, but I can cast a stone across the waters to create many ripples.

~MOTHER TERESA

FOR OVER A DECADE and a half, I have had the good fortune of developing women leaders using the principles that are found in this book. From North America to Europe, to Asia and South America, my team and I have taught influence principles and practices to women that have enabled them to speak up, speak out, ask for what they want, negotiate, and demonstrate they can be leaders who can charge forth strategically as well as care for the people who work for them. These women have become influencers in their organizations and communities and so can you.

As women who lead countries, companies, churches, communities, and homes, we need to influence others every day. Influence turns out to be one of the most foundational competencies to effective leadership in most any context. In other words, we get more done, and enact more effective change by influencing rather than coercing, dictating, or demanding.

I first came to understand the significance of influence as a key ingredient for effective leadership many years ago. At the time I was working as an organizational consultant developing and delivering diversity programs for a multinational client. The emphasis for that client at that time was helping women discover and address the things we as women did that hindered our success in the workplace. For instance, research of that era suggested that we as women talked in ways that hindered our being heard as true leaders. It suggested that we as women were too polite and hesitated to give our opinion until it was our turn to speak. In those days, according to some, our influence as women meant we had to learn ways to adapt to traditional male cultures in the workplace, while striving for balance in our personal lives.

In this client's program, the client targeted women who were at mid-level leadership in the organization but had hit the glass ceiling—the level of leadership above which few women ascended. Interestingly enough, I saw manifestations of this invisible barrier across industries and cultural groups. Women in organized religious life called that leadership threshold the "stained glass ceiling." Some African American women called it the "concrete ceiling," suggesting they as a group weren't close enough to the top to even see possibilities of advancing to the top. Some Asian women called it the "bamboo ceiling," connoting the nuanced gender barriers that many of them faced. Significant for me was when women of different cultural backgrounds were put together in programs to learn new strategies the similarity of our experiences was striking. The power was in coming together and realizing our experiences, though not exactly alike, were not isolated.

To that end, an eye-opening experience occurred for me at the end of a workshop on influence skills that I had led for a group of women leaders in Atlanta. After all the participants had departed, I sat still and reveled in the special moment trying to make sense of what had just occurred. I realized that I, along with twenty-five or so participants, had created something so special it felt as though the magic lingered still after the training had ended. It's as though each of the women had come into my workshop and learned each was not alone in dealing with sexism in her respective company. It's as if I could hear each woman say, "It is not my imagination," "I am not crazy," "I am not alone." And even more powerfully, they left saying, "Now, I have options." They gained the kind of power that comes from a self-revelation that once attained cannot be lost. That was a wake-up call for each of us. The approach to leading I shared was revelatory. Though I had studied all the significant organizational leadership theories in graduate school, I knew the real ahas occur when we create safe spaces for women of different backgrounds to tell their stories, unpack their experiences, and apply frameworks and tools to develop choices for how they will lead. That is the power of influence that starts internally and emanates out to make an impact on others.

We've come a long way. Today, far more women are in leadership roles at significantly higher levels. The intention of this book is to go beyond those early lessons and share the strategies learned by women across the globe so you can successfully use the principles of influence to make a difference wherever you lead. However, at this stage of women's leadership, we can no longer afford to provide models that suggest women merely need to adopt the styles of men to be successful or that we are inherently deficient in our leadership approaches. Effective organizational leadership demands evolution.

For too long, we have listened to experts give us strategies on how to dress for success (which in my early career entailed shoulder-padded, boxy, shapeless suits and floppy bowties, as if we were attempting to be "mini-men"). We have been told to think like a man, interrupt like a man, and compete for the corner office like a man. This advice continues to valorize male models over female models of leadership. And worse—it stereotypes all men into a mold that is unattainable and limiting. Ironically, more research corroborates the value women bring to the workplace, including the bottom line.[1] Once known as "soft skills," and primarily associated with women, collaboration, communication, cultural competence, and influence are now the "hot skills" for success in today's highly matrixed, global work environment—for both men and women.

And let's be honest: organizational leaders must continue to address structures and systems that overlook, over talk, over explain things to, and ultimately, pass over women. More and more, the most effective organizations develop inclusive leadership

1. Gerzema and D'Antonio, *The Athena Doctrine.*

practices that address gender biases (whether conscious or unconscious). Leaders in these organizations understand it is not enough to use more advanced theories of organizations but that they have to cultivate a workplace culture in which diverse styles of leading are valued and includes the wide-ranging styles of women.

Organizations are changing and broadening their talent pools to acquire and advance more women into leadership. Let's face it: women, we are changing the very nature of work. And together we can continue to influence our organizations for the better. In order to influence around us, now is the time for emerging and existing women leaders to do the inside work that will help us influence with authenticity. The work of influence starts inside of each of us and emanates out into our interactions.

The "I" that Influences

Having the ability to make a positive impact on others is really at the heart of what it means to influence. Influence is a verb and a noun. In other words, influence is something you do and something you possess. Influence is action that you take to make impact on others and the organization or community in which you work, live, or serve. It is also the interpersonal and social capital you amass with others that enables you to affect people and environments.

True influence starts from within—knowing the "I" within— your authentic self, sometimes referred to as the "true self," or your God-given selfhood. Parker Palmer describes Rosa Parks, a true influencer, in terms that helps us understand authentic self. "The universal element in her story is not the substance of her fight but the selfhood in which she stood while she fought—for each of us holds the challenge and the promise of naming and claiming true self."[2] Mrs. Parks influenced from a place of internal power and leading from within.

Influence then starts with growing in self-awareness of your purpose, identity, skills, behaviors, and perceptions of your

2. Palmer, *Let Your Life Speak*, 35.

environment. Influence entails leading from an inner place of conviction about your purpose and your belief about the potential of the people around you to effect change for the greater good, as well as knowing who you are, your strengths, your preferences, your values, and your beliefs. Influence encompasses each of us as leaders (or aspiring leaders) understanding our own cultural identity and the impact of how each of us has been socialized, developed, and formed and how that "I" impacts others and even sees others.

I grew up in the foothills of the Allegheny mountains in the tri-state region of Pennsylvania-Ohio-West Virginia. Black people represented about 5 percent of the population, and we were interconnected through our neighborhoods and churches. I attended elementary school in Pennsylvania, high school in Ohio, and worked my first summer jobs in West Virginia—all within a 10-mile or so radius of one another. I completed my college education in Ohio and ultimately earned my doctorate. So meaningful for my community back home was my earning the doctorate that my brother Joe and close friend Helen hosted my graduation party, and nearly every person in the African American community of that region attended. As an offspring of that community, I represented them. As I looked out on that packed banquet hall, I mused, "Not only does it takes a village to raise a child, it takes a village to earn a PhD!" Those were the people who prayed for me, mentored me, encouraged me, and cheered me on. I was connected to them, and any influence I garnered was and is a direct result of the communities from which I hailed and even now belong.

Ubuntu is an African concept that captures this idea quite well. Desmond Tutu defined it this way: The first law of our being is that we are set in a delicate network of interdependence with our fellow human beings and with the rest of God's creation.[3] Influence is wrapped also in this communal interdependent sense of "I." This true identity, interconnected to others, is at the heart of influence for the greater good.

Since the days of my youth and education, I have come to belong to multiple communities from which I've come to understand

3. Tutu, *God Has a Dream*, 25.

and glean insight into the type of leadership based in shared power garnered and used in service for the greater good. My professional career has been anchored in the communities of working women, professional women, preaching women, and academic women.

Defining Influence

Whether leading in the classroom or the boardroom, it's not just how you show up that determines a great deal of the influence you will be able to garner with others; it's also about how you think about showing up. I usually start my workshops by asking women to provide a word or phrase that defines influence for them. Here are some of their insights:

- Bringing people along
- Persuasion
- Gaining agreement
- Trying to get someone to see your point of view
- Getting people on your side
- Bringing people along in a positive attitude
- Engaging other people to gain your objectives
- Building an emotional connection with someone
- Getting someone to trust
- Inspiration
- The ability to get something done
- Integrity
- Mutually beneficial
- Impact
- Respect
- Accountability
- Powerful

- The ability to mentor
- Validate
- Listening
- The ability to relate

These are great words and phrases. They provide insight into how women in those leadership sessions thought about influence—as a personal attribute (something they possess) that enabled them to accomplish goals or make a difference with others (something they do).

Isn't that the heart of influence? Possessing the ability to make a positive impact on others, being mindful of the interconnection with them. Over the years I've come to define influence as the power to effect change or gain commitment in people, teams, or organizations for the good of all. Let's unpack this definition some more.

Influence is power. It's the positive use of power to shape ideas, mindsets, and behavior of people and teams and to better organizations, institutions, and communities. As an influencer you wield power. Mary Parker Follett was a management consultant who wrote and taught in the early twentieth century, way before some of the most noted management gurus today. Parker Follett believed that each member of any group has unique and distinct power—their individuality and contribution needed to be valued. She distinguished between two types of power—"power-over" and "power-with"—and went against the grain of her day by calling for leaders and managers to make a shift from "power-over" tactics to "power-with" tactics.

Parker Follett defined "power-over" as a coercive power of some person or group over some other person or group. She defined "power-with" as a jointly developed power or a power of interactive influence. What she described as "power-with" is at the heart of influence. Influence is a power *with* others, not a power *over* others.[4]

4. Follett, *Prophet of Management*.

Influence is change. Influence is about changing mindsets, behaviors, processes, systems, people, goals—you name it. There would be no need to influence if there was no need for change. As a leader or a leader in the making, you help people change. You help organizations change. But you can't make anyone change. Influence is an approach to change that will help you help others change.

Influence is about gaining commitment. You will only be able to gain commitment to the extent you influence the perspective of others so they see how committing to a specific course of action is in their best interest as well as the best interests of the organization or institution in which they serve. To bring people along for personal or organizational gain in any other way is force and coercion.

Whether at home or work, influence is a powerful approach to get things done, especially when you don't have authority to direct and enforce the actions of others. Most of us would agree that in homes, corporations, community groups, churches, and schools, time's up for a bully approach to leadership in which the will of a leader is forced upon the people he or she leads. To influence effectively, a leader must balance setting goals and achieving outcomes with building and maintaining relationships. Yet influence is much more than a skill set. Influence is an approach to leading or a mindset that helps to grow oneself and other leaders. And that's why it is especially crucial for women leaders now. As more and more women enter organizational life and advance into roles or positions of leadership, the more we must develop and cultivate powerful leadership skills in women coming up the ranks in order to shape our organizations for the good of all.

The Personal Side of Leadership

When I step back and look at my journey in developing women leaders, I am still struck by and thankful for the people who invested in me to help me influence others. While many programs and books address the skill-building side of influence, rarely is there one that addresses the personal side of influence, particularly for women. Here's why it's important:

Women leaders, no matter how senior or experienced, are affected by the embedded threats of racism and sexism, and no matter how strong we are individually, these issues threaten to break us down. While leaders and activists rightfully continue to address the structural and systemic issues facing women, we still need resources that help us build the inner side of our leadership. And having served in leadership in the corporate arena, the academy, and the church, as well as having trained or coached women in those same institutions and others, I can attest that it is helpful to carve out time and space and do the inner work on our leadership, so that we can influence for greater change on behalf of all.

So I write this book with you, the woman leader, in mind—whether you are emerging into leadership or already an existing leader. *Influence Starts with "I"* provides a roadmap for you to build the personal side of leadership that will enable you to gain commitment and effect change for the greater good.

Make a commitment to yourself. Take a personal retreat. Carve out quiet time. Create a buffer from the noise of the day and work on the "I" of your influence. Invite some fellow women leaders to read this book with you. After you've done your journaling and personal work, get with trusted friends to discuss your shared insights. You'll find, as I did many years ago, that when we create that safe space to talk and share, something magical happens.

Here's how this book is laid out:

Chapter 1: Know Your Purpose

To influence and continue to influence, you've got to have a clear sense of purpose. You've got to know what you stand for and why you lead the way you do. Clarity of purpose provides the overarching umbrella or the why of your leadership and helps provide focus to your influence. In this chapter, I will help you articulate your leadership purpose.

Chapter 2: See Yourself as a Leader

How you see yourself is critical to how you will lead and ultimately influence others. I've talked to too many women who just could not see themselves as leaders. They remained stuck where they were and failed to garner the influence to grow and advance. In this chapter, I will provide you with self-awareness tools for developing and declaring your leader identity.

Chapter 3: Lead from Within

What you do as a leader must flow from who you are as a leader: not the who that is projected from a leader mask, but the authentic you that is clear on who she is deep down in the core of her identity. It is from that place of strength that the leader influences and makes a difference in her world. Influence is energized from the power of leading from within. In this chapter, I will show you the key to leading from within.

Chapter 4: Develop an Influence Mindset

An influence mindset is the ability to think strategically and positively about your goals and aspirations in light of the goals and aspirations of others. An influence mindset enables you to shift your thinking from winning over to winning with others. The influence mindset is key to owning your own power while respecting the power of others, all in service to the greater good. In this chapter, I'll help you cultivate an influence mindset.

Chapter 5: Boost Your Confidence

Did you know that confidence equates with success as much as if not more than competence? You will need to be competent in your chosen leadership vocation. And you will need to possess and display confidence so others come to trust your expertise and experience. In this chapter, I help you identify your confidence boosters so you can face situations with self-assurance.

Chapter 6: Use Your Power Strategically

You have power: your own power and the collective power of other women and men who serve as your allies, advocates, and associates. In organizational and community life, you have multiple types of power. In this chapter, I will help you own and leverage all of your power for greater influence.

Chapter 7: Negotiate Barriers

Your greatest gift in influencing is you. As a woman leader, some of the greatest barriers to your influence are barriers associated with your identity. Such barriers are the conscious and unconscious biases through which others see and judge your leadership. Still in this day and age, stereotypes abound and can hinder you from influencing and making impact if you are not mindful. In this chapter, I give you strategies for navigating these barriers.

Chapter 8: Develop Your Support System

Every great influencer does so from a base of support. That support comes from your network—the collection of personal and professional relationships that provide the foundation for your influence. But your network doesn't just emerge from nowhere. You must be intentional in cultivating and contributing to it. In this chapter, I provide you with tools to examine and strengthen your network.

Chapter 9: Recognize Everyday Opportunities to Influence

To influence, you have got to become accustomed to recognizing and then leveraging the opportunities you see. In some ways, the best influencers create opportunities. However, let's face it: it's not always in the large change processes that we truly shape the world around us but in our daily interactions. It is from the daily opportunities to influence that the greater influence emerges.

Chapter 10: Plan Your Path Forward

In the final chapter, I provide a call to action for you. You have goals and aspirations that honing your influence can help with. It's now time for you to make your mark. You can do it. Influence starts with your willingness to see yourself as a leader, own and strategically use your purpose and power, build your network, and develop an influence mindset.

We must continue to open the dialogue between women and men on the topic of leadership. This book can help do that. The gender dynamics I address in several chapters are informative for both men and women, and because influence is not a competency that only women need to develop, I invite men to read this book as well. But please read it through the lens that I am speaking to women as I share the stories of women and male allies from across the world. Consequently, I have maintained the use of the feminine pronoun. In sharing some women's stories, I have changed their names to protect confidentiality and position the stories more broadly to draw generalized lessons from them.

Whether you work in a corporate setting or a non-profit organization, you can grow your influence so that your voice (and by extension your ideas) can be heard more clearly. The influence that starts with "I" can help you shape the ideas and thoughts of those you work with, as well as help you bring about positive change in your organization.

Let's get started on this influence journey.

Put It into Action

On a separate sheet of paper, draw a timeline of your influence journey. Note specific periods of your life and how the events and people of that time period influenced you. Based on where you've been and where you'd like to go, write out an influence goal statement that starts with I.

My influence goal: I will . . .

Reflection/Discussion Questions

1. How might the development of influence help you in your professional life? How might it help you in your personal life?

2. What were some of the experiences in your early life that influenced you?

3. Who were some key people who helped support you in your development as a leader? Exactly how did they influence you?

1

Know Your Purpose

The purpose of leadership is not to make the present bearable. The purpose of leadership is to make the future possible.

~JOAN D. CHITTISER

JOI WAS A MID-LEVEL Chinese American manager in a large health care system. She managed a large department and took pride in developing the men and women who reported to her. One day she shared this with me: "I develop people well and give them great exposure—from which a number of my direct reports have been promoted and given their next opportunity." She went on to say, "Sadly, no one is doing that for me."

How many of us as women have felt similarly? We hunker down and do the work, taking care of tasks and projects like "dutiful daughters," exceeding expectations, expecting decision makers to recognize our efforts and promote us. We cannot relegate our career success or our influence into the hands of others. Each of us must be clear on our individual purpose and prepared to move forward purposefully.

When Joi had first come to me, she seemed to think she was constrained by her cultural values. She said, "Jeanne, the things you teach about speaking up and sharing my successes with people in my organization go against my cultural values." Of course, I assured her I would never want her to do anything that violated her cultural values. So I explored more with her, wanting to get a better sense of her cultural values. That's when she shared with me that no one in her organization seemed to do for her what she was doing for members of her team—helping them to advance and succeed.

Not wanting to assume I knew the values of her culture, I asked her what were the cultural values that informed her work. Without hesitating, she emphatically replied, "I'm Catholic!" Imagine my surprise to hear that, as I was thinking it was the values of her ethnic culture that were driving her consternation. Joi's story reminds us not to stereotype people based on our own assumptions and to also be sensitive to the intersecting identities that comprise who we are.

So I asked her to consider that she had a set of values and also worked in an organization that had a culture and values that defined and promoted a set of leaders that exhibited those values and advanced the cause of the institution. I asked her to think about whether or not she could adapt to the organization's cultural values without violating her own. "For instance," I asked her, "if you travelled to another country whose culture was different than your own, would you not find ways to adapt without abandoning your own values?"

At that moment, a light bulb must have gone off inside her imagination because she animatedly exclaimed, *"Oh, I get it! If I believe I am in my organization to help people, then the higher I go, the more people I can help!"* What an insight.

What Joi was grappling with was a lack of clarity of purpose. Once she articulated and framed her purpose in terms that made sense to her, it released her to adopt strategies that apprised organizational leaders of her accomplishments. Her newly articulated sense of purpose freed her to advance in order to help others become the best they could be—all in a corporate health-care system dedicated to helping people become and remain healthy.

A clear sense of purpose provides the overarching umbrella, or the why of your leadership, and helps provide focus to your influence. Purpose articulates why you do what you do the way you do it.

What Purpose Is Not

At any time in our careers, each of us has worked in specific jobs for a variety of reasons not necessarily related to our overall purpose, including the following:

- To pay bills
- To meet expectations of others (e.g., parents, spouse, partner, etc.)
- To gain needed skills
- To make a living

All of these are necessary reasons for working, yet they are transactional reasons. They help you complete the transaction of a job or position, but they don't provide an overarching reason that transforms a job into a career and calling or a role into true leadership. For that you need purpose—specifically leadership purpose.

I believe because each of us was created for a purpose, we are programed for purpose. Consequently, humans have a need to find meaning in what we do because of that ingrained desire for purpose.

Hermina Ibarra and her research partners wrote about leadership purpose and its role in women's leadership development. According to Ibarra and her partners, people become leaders by internalizing a leadership identity and developing a sense of purpose. "A person asserts leadership by taking purposeful action."[1]

Noted leadership coach and author Kevin Cashman defines purpose as "your unique meaningful contribution" that serves "the needs of others."[2] For me purpose is how what you do from your passion and values helps meet the needs of others. Purpose is your mission on earth and in your corner of the world.

Purpose is greater than the sum of your daily tasks. Purpose is more than your job title, role, or position in the company or organization you work for. Purpose helps to align all the various

1. Ibarra, Ely, and Kolb, *Women Rising*, 3.
2. Cashman, *Leadership from the Inside Out*, 67.

components of your life (work, home, community) into an integrated whole that provides coherence to what you do in any given context at any given time. Your purpose is the reason you exist and lead the way you do.

I was facilitating a cohort of emerging leaders in my WIELD™ (Women's Initiative for Emerging Leaders' Development) program. To be in the program, each woman had been selected and supported by her executive leader as an up-and-coming leader. Each had significant responsibility, leading sizable departments and teams. As part of developing their talent pipeline in the technology organization they worked for, these women were being groomed and given opportunities to compete for senior leadership roles. Some entered the program with the notions that, in their current role, their purpose was either to make their boss look good or eventually to take over their boss's job.

Both of these notions are commendable but too narrow and myopic to help women advance to more senior roles or garner the influence they need to make an impact on their part of the world. To begin to get them thinking more broadly about what they did and why, I helped each of them develop a leadership purpose statement.

A leadership purpose statement is nothing more than a purpose statement for leaders. It is a statement that clarifies why a person leads, and it integrates a leader's sense of leadership across various domains of her life. At work it provides grounding for one's leadership role. Ultimately, it opens possibilities for leading that transcend merely advancing up the designated corporate or institutional ladder.

This statement expresses your why for doing what you do the way you do it. Your leadership purpose transcends any one given position or organization, but it frames the thing to which you are connected—even called to—in order to serve and help others. Your leadership purpose may be fulfilled in your organization. When you come to articulate that purpose, your thinking around roles that you fit or can fulfill shifts.

After going through the reflection work to write out her leadership purpose, one emerging leader in that WIELD™ cohort admitted that "it was certainly jolting but empowering to find this purpose within me." She was a manager for a global technology firm, and her responsibility was to oversee the management of the hardware and software assets. Yet when she took the time to reflect on and write out her purpose statement, she wrote:

> My leadership purpose is "to strategize, prioritize, and plan for growth, evolvement and success of the organization, to guide and support others and to act with honesty, integrity amid transparency for the greater good."

As you see, this purpose transcends her current role or even the goal of achieving the next level in the organization. This purpose focuses this leader toward strategizing and prioritizing growth for the greater good as her values of honesty, integrity, and transparency drive her. This purpose can be lived out at work or at home, and in any organization or institution. It is fundamental to who this person is and what she does as a leader. And because she is clear on her purpose, her current leadership assignment is a vital place for living her purpose.

Another emerging leader in the cohort who was working as a technical support manager saw her leadership purpose as the following: *to offer a vision of what's possible, unleash potential, and empower people so they can thrive.* What struck her was how consistent her purpose had been throughout her life and career. She wrote to me, "From being a big sister, to leadership roles in school, to D&I efforts at all my organizations and volunteer work, that purpose has been a guiding star."

She went on to share with me, "The exercise with its guiding questions was extremely valuable because it forced us to take the sometimes-vague feelings that we have about who we are and what we do into a clear, articulate message we can remind ourselves and articulate to others." That, my friend, is the power of knowing your purpose. The ability to coalesce your passion, values, and identity into a coherent statement enables you to influence from a place of purpose.

The Leadership Purpose Statement

In the work I do with emerging women leaders, I take them through a series of exercises to write out their leadership purpose statement.

First and foremost, a leadership purpose is need-directed. Purpose reflects a reason for meeting a need that exists. A leadership purpose statement then will reflect meeting some need. People have needs; and you have skills, abilities, gifts, and experiences to meet some of those needs. Though purpose transcends the workplace, surely it is a place to bring your purpose to bear in addressing needs where you work. Therefore, a leadership purpose statement conveys that some group or population is helped by your leadership. At its heart leadership is about relationship, and influence is the power of leaders to effect change through relationships. Knowing the types of needs you are called to address keeps you focused.

Next, a leadership purpose statement will be values-based. A leadership purpose statement is fueled by passion and reflects your core values. You bring core values to work every day, and these values give life to your leadership and influence. Finally, leadership purpose is active. Influencers are often agents of change—actively working toward the greater good. A leadership purpose statement reflects the actions provided by your leadership.

At the end of this chapter, I provide you with a template to write out your leadership purpose statement. But there are a few things you need to do before you get started.

Preparing for Purpose

Make an appointment with yourself. Schedule time on your calendar to sit with your thoughts and reflect on your passions, values, and purpose. Block out the time. If you are like too many leaders I work with, your organizations are hyper busy and offer little time for reflection or even strategic thinking. You must make this a priority. Your ability to influence depends on it. It depends on you finding the "I" within you and articulating the driving passions and purpose that transcend a role or job.

Take a notebook or journal and write out the common themes of your leadership in a variety of contexts over the past three to five years. In addition to your leadership at work, think about your home life, your volunteer work in the community, and your service in your faith community. Identify the common themes.

I remember shortly after completing my doctoral studies and working as a tenure-track professor at a local university, I pulled out a stenographer's notebook and started writing. I didn't have a fancy journal. The word that kept coming to me was *development*. Developing was a common thread of what I had done up to that point—whether at work as an organizational development consultant helping professionals grow, as a minister guiding others toward faith development, or working with community groups on personal and team development. A basic study of development led me to see that my purpose was to help people, teams, and organizations grow, mature, and ultimately become more effective. Growth was a core value; as an influencer, catalyzing others to grow or develop was an action I embraced. My leadership purpose was to move people and systems to higher levels of effectiveness. I live that out through my company as that purpose statement is our tagline, but I live it out personally also. That purpose statement freed me to use my skills and gifts in diverse contexts. Even now it helps me focus my energies and does not limit me to any one place or cause.

Now it's your turn. It is time for you to get started. Know your purpose so you influence authentically, passionately, and clearly.

Put It into Action

Elements of a Leadership Purpose Statement

- Need-directed—a leadership purpose statement conveys that some group or population is helped by your leadership. What is your why for doing what you do the way you do it?
- Values-based: a leadership purpose statement is fueled by passion and reflects your core values. What core values do you bring to work every day that give life to your leadership?
- Active—a leadership purpose statement reflects the distinct action or activities provided by your leadership. What action words reflect your leadership?

My leadership purpose is to

_____

(action word(s) that reflect your leadership)

_____

_____

(your core values)

to, for, or with

_____

(a group or population)

Pull it Together:

In the space below, craft your leadership purpose statement by connecting the above three sections. You may rewrite and tweak the wording of the statement to suit your style.

Reflection/Discussion Questions

1. As you look at this statement, what strikes you or particularly catches your attention about the statement?

2. What feelings does this statement evoke in you?

3. In what ways does it reflect themes from throughout your life?

4. How does this statement convey who you are and what you stand for? How does it frame your current leadership? And potentially your future leadership?

——— 2 ———

See Yourself as a Leader

Our self-perception determines our behavior. If we think we're small, limited, inadequate creatures, then we tend to behave that way, and the energy we radiate reflects those thoughts no matter what we do. If we think we're magnificent creatures with an infinite abundance of love and power to give, then we tend to behave that way. Once again, the energy around us reflects our state of awareness.

~MARIANNE WILLIAMSON

YEARS AGO, WHILE CONDUCTING an extensive research project in a South Carolina sea island community, I met a talented African American professional named Nadine. While Nadine was involved in various civic and business organizations—primarily to build her network and strengthen her connections—she wasn't really involved in her own community. As a matter of fact, she was often the only black woman involved in those organizations. However, her involvement with that small South Carolina sea island community changed a lot for her.

Large corporate entities were purchasing prime waterfront property and displacing the Gullah people and the culture native to the region. Enlisting members of the community to get involved in the fight to preserve their community, activists in collaboration with the Penn Center created a training program to equip participants with leadership skills and invited Nadine to join them. Nadine accepted the invitation and ended up gaining more than just a new set of skills. She developed a new sense of her identity as a leader and her ability to influence others and situations for positive change. Nadine described the development program as "an eye-opening experience."

You see, prior to that extensive community training program, though active in her profession, Nadine had never seen herself as a leader. She didn't believe she could influence others and make a difference. The program helped bolster her sense of self and ultimately changed her life. She discovered her own giftedness and learned new skills. Nadine recognized that she had something to offer her own community, and she was able to use her skills to network and build relationships with other people to help transform the sea island community. By the end of the program, her eyes were opened to not only view others differently but also to see herself as a leader. More so, Nadine was pleasantly surprised to learn that many people in her community already viewed her as a leader.

An eye-opening experience may startle, surprise, or astonish a person. In the case of leadership, it's that sense of astonishment, or of being startled, that actually causes a person to move ever so slightly but definitely toward a vision of her own leadership potential. The eye opener not only causes a person to see herself differently, but also to see others differently and to see circumstances from a new perspective of agency.

Until you have an eye-opening experience about your own leadership, you won't garner the influence you could and should have. Other research bears this out. Whether you lead in a corporation, a church, or a community, there is a "fragile process of coming to see oneself as a leader, and to be seen by others as a leader."[1] Leaders influence. Becoming a leader who influences is more than acquiring new skills, or adapting to the demands of a new role. According to organizational researchers, becoming a leader "involves a fundamental identity shift."[2]

1. Ibarra, Ely, and Kolb, *Women Rising*, 4.
2. Ibid, 4.

Identity

How you see yourself is critical to what you can do as an influencer. It shapes how others see you and the credibility you establish with them.

We each have multiple overlapping identities. Nadine was an African American woman and a professional. As such, these overlaps created distinct experiences for her, as our own identities do for each of us. Nadine shared with me that though she was involved in various civic and professional organizations, the relationships she maintained with others in those predominantly white organizations were superficial. She didn't see the real people because she dealt with them solely on a professional level and conversely, she surmised they didn't see the real person in her.

The make-up of the leadership training program was very diverse—consisting of women and men of various races, including participants of the Historical Preservation Society and the Sea Island Preservation Society. There were many activities in the program that helped bolster Nadine's sense of herself, but one stood out for her: the diversity training module. Through that experience, Nadine saw that people from different backgrounds possessed different values. It helped her to examine how African American women see things differently from European American women, and how white men see things differently from black men. She learned that value systems differed by race and gender and not everyone assumed or thought about things the way she did as an African American woman or as a unique individual.

The program prompted Nadine to reflect on her professional involvements. She came to realize that she interacted with white people from a set of fixed assumptions that were never challenged because the relationships remained superficial. The interaction in her community leadership school challenged her assumptions and caused a shift in her thinking. She began to see others differently. The experience was eye opening for her for another reason.

In one of the modules, the class was divided into four groups (black women, black men, white women, white men) and asked a series of questions. The groups were to discuss their answers and later report out to the entire group. One of the questions was "Who are your heroes and heroines, and why?" It was an awakening for Nadine to hear from people in her affinity group that several people whom she had known all her life but did not interact with much saw her as a heroine. When she looked at herself, she saw just another person. To those neighbors, Nadine was someone who had made it and was successfully navigating the business world. It was through that exercise that she discovered others already viewed her as a leader. Again, it shifted her perspective about herself and opened her eyes to another facet of her own identity.

Coming to see oneself as a leader is necessary for leading authentically and influencing for impact. In many ways, "leader" becomes a thread that runs through the overlapping identities we hold. As a black woman who had previously not been so connected to her own African American community, Nadine's newly acquired leader identity moved her to collaborate with other leaders from outside her community to protect their island. That leader identity also gave Nadine a new set of lenses through which to see the issues of her community and gave her a sense of calling, purpose, and responsibility to effect change in it.

Whether you lead in a corporation, a community agency, or a faith-based institution, developing your leader identity is critical to your being able to influence and effect positive change. Developing this sense of identity is not an event, but it is an eye-opening process of growth, reexamined assumptions, and self-empowerment.

So how do you come to see yourself as a leader?

Examine Your Lenses

My experiences in training and coaching women leaders suggest that assertive or strong women are generally regarded as pushy or aggressive; that women aren't expected to excel at math or science; and that many people, especially from some faith traditions, still believe that a woman's place is in the home. These unfounded beliefs are held by men *and* women.

For instance, at some point in the not-too-distant past, a study in the Philippines found that 54 percent of female respondents believed that women who worked were pushy.[3] And according to Harvard's gender Implicit Association Test (IAT),[4] both men and women the world over associate men more than women with science and having a career. In fact, 75 percent of male respondents to the IAT display the automatic gender stereotype of "male = work" and "female = family." Eighty percent of women show the same automatic stereotype.[5] These statistics illustrate a stereotype about professional women held by men and, surprisingly, by women as well, that can limit women's views of ourselves.

Too often, women have internalized gender bias against females, and we collude with a sexist system that holds other women back. When you encounter gender bias in your organization, make sure to examine and challenge your own assumptions about your and other women's gifts and abilities. The way you see gender and leadership could actually be one of the things holding you back.

Now don't get me wrong, there are plenty of conscious and unconscious biases that we face from others—especially in male-dominated systems. Other people's stereotypes don't have to become a barrier to your success. I share more with you in chapter seven on navigating those barriers.

For now, examine the lens through which you see and interpret yourself.

Envision Yourself at the Front of the Room

Kiara worked as a summer intern for me before starting her senior year in college. A communications and media studies major, her internship entailed editing scripts and video footage for my company's social media platforms. Because I believe it is important to mentor younger women in leadership and not just provide

3. P&G, Pantene Philippines #WhipIt Campaign Goes Global Virally
4. https://implicit.harvard.edu/implicit/
5. Banaji and Greenwald, *Blindspot*, 115.

tasks to complete, I secured permission from one of my clients for Kiara to join me for a training session of a women's leadership cohort I was training. Kiara came along to help me set up, take notes on the teaching and observe women leaders from around the globe in action.

During one of the breakout sessions, in which the cohort members were working on a reflection activity, I walked to the back of the room where Kiara was seated and asked her if she was enjoying the session. She immediately responded with how much she was benefitting from the session. I replied, "Great, it is important for you to see a woman of color at the front of the room leading a session for women leaders. In fact, I want you to be able to see yourself at the front of the room one day." Her smile lit up her face as she reflected on that. She then said, "I can see myself one day at the head of the table reviewing scripts with my writing team!"

The image Kiara created and now carries in her mind will help move her toward leading. Clearly, she will continue to prepare and develop the necessary acumen for her field. She will build a network and develop a strong mentoring relationship, but the possibilities for leading are even greater now that she can see herself leading. As the saying goes, "If you can see it, you can be it."

Take Note of What Others See in You

Note when others see leadership potential in you. Then look a little deeper and accept it. Larraine was a customer service agent for a large package delivery company. Her manager saw leadership potential in her by the professionalism with which she handled customers and the influence she already had garnered with other team members. However, when he told her he wanted to promote her to supervisor of a team, she balked. She just couldn't see it! Her manager persisted. Larraine talked it over with me, and I encouraged her to go for it. After more reflection and much consternation, she did. Now twenty-three years later, Larraine has continued to advance in management and leads the company's initiatives for launching new systems and the international training of those systems. Larraine's manager and coaching helped her to look a little deeper into her own self.

Who has approached you about a leadership role or advancement to senior leadership? Don't reject it. Take a risk and at least talk to that person about the opportunity. Don't let fear hold you back.

Pay Attention

Pay attention to the influence you have already garnered. Note the times you call follow-up meetings with your team. Pay attention to the times when you synthesize takeaways in meetings. In those small, everyday interactions, you are demonstrating your leadership and influence. Others are taking note. Are you? Pay attention to the times people look to you for wisdom or movement.

Shift Your Perspective

Notice where you practice leadership in specific venues such as community work or volunteer roles, and shift your perspective to more fully own your leadership in the workplace. For instance, Tonya worked in a pretty mundane customer service role for a large company. Always the achiever, she was passionately involved in her children's school. She was elected to the school board and had worked diligently to lead efforts at education reform—even after her children had long graduated from the school system. Recently, Tonya's position in her company was eliminated. Through her extensive network, Tonya was recommended for and landed a similar role in another company. Within months, her new manager recognized the leadership potential in her and recrafted her job description to lead major projects for the company.

Think about where you have been exercising leadership and influencing others and how those experiences and skills can be transferred to your current professional context.

Expand Your View of Leadership

Words are carriers of meaning. Sometimes what hinders some of us from potentially seeing ourselves as leaders is the way "leader" has been defined by us or others in our organizations. How we view or understand a concept depends on the inherent meaning our culture has invested in this word. Leader in too many ways is still very male-laden. It has a long history of being male identified, from the ancient Greek hero myths to the images of hard-charging military leaders. Studies suggest that even in some of today's corporations, senior male executives associate strong leadership with widely held beliefs about male behavior.[6]

Begin to define "leadership" more holistically, as a process of moving others forward. That process takes interpersonal and strategic abilities. See a leader as someone who directs and guides; who gives direction and listens; who cares for the people she leads, the organization she stewards, and the bottom line over which she is accountable.

As one very senior executive leader reflecting back on her career shared with me, "*I saw myself as a leader first. Then the strengths and experiences I brought as a woman were my difference that I leveraged or brought to the table.*" Being able to see yourself as a leader is crucial to you becoming a leader. Being able to see yourself as a leader is crucial to you developing the influence mindset that will help you make a difference around you.

6. PWC, *Mending the Gender Gap*, 8.

Put It Into Action

Identify three to five trusted advisors, mentors, confidantes, and friends who know you well in your professional or personal setting. Ask each of them the following questions:

1. What leadership capacity have you seen in me?
2. From what you've observed, what five words best describe my passions?

Use the following worksheet to summarize the conversations.

	Person 1	Person 2	Person 3
Leadership capacity seen in me:			
Descriptor 1:			
Descriptor 2:			
Descriptor 3:			
Descriptor 4:			
Descriptor 5:			

	Person 4	Person 5	
Leadership capacity seen in me:			
Descriptor 1:			
Descriptor 2:			
Descriptor 3:			
Descriptor 4:			
Descriptor 5:			

Reflection/Discussion Questions

1. What themes do you see from the worksheet summary? What surprises you about these themes? What in these themes is confirmation for you?

2. How do you define leader for your professional (or community) context?

3. In what ways do the themes from the above activity align with your definition of leader? In what ways do they not align? What does this suggest to you?

3

Lead from Within

"The most effective way to lead is to lead from within."

~ LOLLY DASKAL

ONE OF MY GREATEST lessons on influence actually came as a result of a series of mistakes I made. It occurred in my very first influence training session for executive women leaders.

I had completed the first phase of my training with my certifying trainer, Kira, and was scheduled to lead my first seminar in Dallas. I prepared like crazy—reviewing my notes, reading the facilitator's manual, developing my stories, and reviewing the video on gender communication rituals that I considered to be the cornerstone of the course. I arrived early the day before my big workshop, as that next day was critically important and I wanted to have plenty of time to get settled and be mentally prepared to facilitate. If my session was successful, I would receive my certification as a master trainer—which not only meant the possibility of more business but also an opportunity to take my passion for empowering women for leadership and service to a broader audience.

In my diligence to prepare thoroughly for the session up until I was to leave for the airport, I left both my facilitator manual and the video, which was core to the program, back in my home office in Chicago. Of course, I didn't discover my mistake until I was in my hotel room. To put it in greater perspective, it was back in the day before we could stream training videos directly from the distributors or save facilitator's guide on our iPads. Needless to say,

I was aghast. How could I have been so absentminded? All kinds of crazy thoughts attacked me—"You are going to mess this up," "You are going to live out somebody's stereotype of black women not being prepared," "How are you going to face this executive audience with no notes?"

I first called two close friends who were (and still are) crucial members of my support team and asked them to pray. They knew how important the session was to me and my fledgling consulting practice. Later, when I told Kira what I had done, she placed her hand on mine and said,

> We'll get through this! First of all, let me allay your fears. You know this material inside and out. You have years of experience and formal training. Please don't get hung up on not having the facilitator's manual! We'll get through this. The video is a good addition to the program, but you could teach the same points and lead an interactive discussion.

She calmly assured me that I already had *within* me what it took to successfully impact the women who had come to this workshop. Though nervous, I hoped in my heart I could do that, and we began to do what many experienced trainers learn early in our careers: "design on the fly." I prepared to start the workshop, and Kira went to call her East Coast company to see if there was even a remote possibility of getting another video delivered by lunchtime.

Fifteen minutes before the session was to begin, Monty, the executive who had recommended me for the program (which was her corporate baby), stopped me. In my head, I just knew she had heard about my fiasco and was coming to talk about it. But before I could tell her what was going on, she asked me a question that would change the course of my thinking about that day—and the entire program. "Jeanne, I've been meaning to ask you something. You're a Christian, aren't you?"

I looked at her in amazement, as I'm not typically asked that question in diversity and inclusion circles. Monty, a white woman, took inclusion to another level by bringing in the faith component.

I responded, "Why, yes I am." She moved closer as if she were about to reveal a girl-hood secret. "I thought so! I know we have placed high expectation on you to get ready for this new program, and we have a lot riding on its success. I just wanted you to know that I've been praying for you." The very woman I was afraid of disappointing because of her rank and title was praying for my success! Monty and I came from different racial groups but had this in common: we believed in the power of leading from within based on our faith and calling to make a difference.

I then let her know what was going on and asked her to continue to pray. You can only imagine how I felt as I opened the session for those executive-level women. I was nervous that I did not have my familiar trainer's trappings and had to make do with newly generated notes, yet I felt peace that so much prayer was going on for me and my lessons for the women that day were deeply embedded within my heart ready to burst out. Monty's timing proved to be a strategic reminder to me that I had a God-given purpose to lead women and help them grow their own influence and leadership wherever they were called to serve or work.

So, without a facilitator's guide or a video, I drew on my years of teaching gender and communication in university courses and on the notes I did have to conduct the training, improvising as I went along and trusting the process I was in. I drew upon an internal power in ways I may not have, if I had all the training trinkets at my fingertips. I shared the frameworks for the workshop but highlighted them with the stories that no facilitator manual could have given me. The leader within me came forth in ways that were powerful and memorable.

The Leader Within You

There, too, is a leader inside of you waiting to be awakened. If she is already "woke," then that leader within is ready to influence for the greater good. Knowing who you are deep inside, and leading from that authentic place, is ultimately the key to your ability to influence others.

You were created with inner qualities that make you the unique person you are and the distinct leader you are becoming. You also developed characteristics as you were socialized in your childhood, at school, in your neighborhood, and possibly your faith community. You've come to hold on to certain beliefs and values that drive your behavior in ways that are distinctly you. Because of your skills, abilities, inner gifts, and experiences, you are developing into a leader like no other. No one can lead like you—and you should not try to lead like anyone else.

Role models help us recognize the leadership gifts in ourselves, but they must not be the pattern we try to imitate in order to be effective, successful leaders. Leading from within entails leading from the strength of your inner qualities that make you distinct rather than from a leadership script imposed from outside of yourself.

What are the inner qualities that make you distinct?

Your Personality

You were born and shaped with a personal style that, like your fingerprint, is yours and yours alone. That imprinting shapes how you lead yourself and lead others.

Early on in my career, I was asked to take the Myers-Briggs Type Indicator (MBTI). There are many tools available today to codify your personality and personal style. I happen to still like the MBTI. My results from using that instrument helped me to appreciate my gregarious, intuitive, people-oriented, flexible style. My style was often vastly different from the other people I worked with, yet an understanding of personal style helped me to allow my distinctives to shine forth without trying to hide them behind some mask. Recognizing and appreciating my own style allowed me to continue to seek opportunities that were aligned with how I was shaped. And while others around me may not have always appreciated my style, my understanding of my own style helped me not to be intimidated by theirs.

Your Passion

I graduated from college with a degree in industrial and systems engineering and went to work as a logistics engineer in a pharmaceutical company in Columbus, Ohio, right after graduation. My very first project was to manage the design, build, and implementation of an inventory control system for the warehouse that stocked and distributed educational literature that accompanied the company's health products.

The project entailed me working with the senior leaders of the major departments (sales, marketing, warehouse operations, etc.) to determine their needs for the system and develop the specs for the system. There I was a 22-year-old black woman facilitating spec meetings with senior white men who yelled at each other to get their point across and ensure their department's needs for the system were a priority. I remember at one point just sitting in one of the meetings feeling like I had landed in the twilight zone. Then I woke up and raised my voice over the men to get their attention and bring some order to the chaos. What they didn't know was that for two summers right out of high school I worked for my father as a safety engineering intern in a refractories plant. I had to go into the plant three to four times a day and climb onto the big stamping machines to get clay samples. Any time we were in the plant, we had to yell over the huge machines to be heard. Thus, I wasn't afraid of a little yelling.

My first project also entailed writing computer code to develop the system. I had done fine in my inventory control class in college and had learned to solve the complex problems. But programming computers? Not only was I not a good coder, but I would lose my focus and get so drowsy sitting at that computer poring over code. I'd have to get up and take a break and go talk to a few colleagues I had met in another department. Compared to sitting in my cubicle trying to figure out code, facilitating the boisterous meetings with the senior leaders actually became the highlight of the project.

Eventually, my manager realized I could not code that system, so he arranged to hire a contract programmer. I'm not sure if the contract programmer was supposed to be mentoring me in coding or if I was to be supervising him, but each day we sat side-by-side in my cubicle while I watched him write and test code. I remember feeling embarrassed that we had to bring someone in to do what I "should have" known how to do. I began to quietly map out my exit strategy.

The system got built, and then it was up to me to train the users on the system. I remember my first training class. I went out to the warehouse and set up training classes for the warehouse workers in charge of managing and picking product inventory. Eureka! That felt so right. I had tapped into a passion—a passion for helping others learn. My passion to develop learning systems evolved into my leadership niche. I suppose I could have asked my manager if I could take additional programming classes and eventually continue to manage in the technical arena—but that path just did not seem to fit me. I followed the path that was aligned to my inner passions and purpose. That's what you'll need to do, too. Look deep within and discover the passions you hold and how those passions can fuel what you do where you are.

Your Principles

Principles and values are beliefs that we each hold dear, are often deeply programmed within us, and guide our lives and leadership. Values emanate from our culture, our family, or country of origin, but they become personal when we take them in and make them ours.

We place value on many things but core principles are those non-negotiable values that help to shape our identity and allow us to live out of that deep sense of who we are. Being asked to give up a core principle places stress on our very being. As one executive leader once told me, "When you find alignment between your values and the goals of the organization, you will find a path upward." The leader within is driven by those inner qualities that shape the real you. And it is only from that authentic place where you can truly influence the world around you for the greater good.

Meet Your Authentic Self

In working with women leaders now for almost thirty years, I've come to really believe that each of us becomes the best leader we can be when we lead from a place of authenticity. Who we are must drive what we do. Or put another way, anything you do as a leader must spring from who you are.

When you lead from your true self, you unleash a type of power that energizes you and those around you. There is a power of leading from within that once unleashed is transformative for you and others around you. Unfortunately, circumstances and organizations in which we work sometimes cause us to hide that true self. Like dressing up at Halloween, we don a mask to become the type of leader we think our organizations and institutions desire and reward. We assimilate to the demands and expectations set forth by our environment; we assimilate to fit in. In fact, in a graduate course I took, the instructor intimated that successful leaders assimilated to the culture of the company in which they worked, and he admonished us to "check our differences at the door." For many women of my generation, checking our differences at the door was code for "you have to assimilate to the male environment from which this culture sprung and is maintained." And you can imagine as a gregarious (translation: outspoken) African American woman, checking my outward difference at the door was not an option, and checking my inner differences at the door was just as difficult, even stifling. So much of who I am personality- and character-wise stems from my gender, ethnicity, faith, and culture.

Not too long ago, I was leading a workshop for emerging leaders in the London office of a global consulting firm. The senior human resources leader stopped by to provide the introduction and welcome to the twenty-five or so women who had convened for an all-day workshop. There she stood, this senior leader, in all her fabulousness. Tall, stately, and chic, she was dressed in a purple sheath dress and purple patent leather peep-toe shoes, and looked as if she belonged in a fashion show instead of a corporate office. And as she encouraged the women to remain present in the workshop that I was about to lead, she encouraged them to really think about who they were and what contribution they were to make to the organization. "Too often," she continued, "we as women work hard to fit into other people's expectations, and we don't bring our full selves to work." Only by bringing our full selves to wherever we lead, unmasked, unfettered, can we truly unleash the power that is stored within us to fulfill our purpose or reason for being where we are and working toward positive change for all.

I recently had a conversation with a senior leader in a financial organization who had retired a few months earlier. She was launching her own coaching business as she had for most of her career helped other women in the workplace. She was volunteering in youth mentoring organizations, and she excitedly proclaimed to me, "I was always a church goer, but I have now found a new church and I'm getting involved in their community and justice projects." As she described her new ventures, she kept interjecting, "I feel like I can finally be myself!" I could hear the serenity in her voice.

That, my friend, is the dilemma for leading in some organizations and institutions. Too many of us have had to armor up to survive the madness of the corporate and institutional world! And too many of you are merely surviving and not thriving.

So how do you tap into the power of leading from within?

Take some time to look within and do the inner work necessary to discover and define your inner leader. Discover and define for yourself, first and foremost, the qualities of your personality— your strengths and your blind spots. My car has an indicator that lights up whenever I am driving and another vehicle enters into my blind spot. Discover your inner indicator that informs you when you are leading from a blind spot and missing important data—especially about people who are different from you. The best way to recognize a blind spot is to seek and accept feedback on your behavior and its effect on others. Go first to the trusted members of your personal support circle and seek feedback.

Get comfortable with naming your passion. Know what excites and inspires you, and at some level, what you feel called to. As women, too many of us in our early days responded affirmatively to the voices around us that told us who we were to be and how we could conform to the acceptable "good girl" standard. Too many of us failed to respect our own voices. To lead authentically, you have to get comfortable with your own inner voice. Some of us cultivate that inner voice through spiritual practices and faith traditions that don't silence women's voices. But now it is time to get accustomed to your own voice. If you listen closely enough, that voice will let you know when you are on the right path.

As a business owner who departed from the corporate arena to follow my passion into consulting and leadership development, I understand how passion fuels entrepreneurs. As a ministry leader in my faith tradition, I know how passion fuels ministers. But I also know men and women whose passions enable them to work and serve in organizations and institutions that enable them and others to do a lot of good in this world.

Figure out how your passion aligns with the products or services of your company or institution. Figure out your core values and guiding principles. You have values that guide your life and leadership that are probably non-negotiable. Too often in our busy hectic lives we fail to take the time to examine what is really important to us.

It's time for you to remove the mask, look within, and get acquainted with your authentic self. Leading from that inner place frees you from having to squeeze into a mold that doesn't really fit. It unleashes an energy in you that ripples out and energizes others. That is the beginning of influence.

Put It into Action

Take a personality inventory that will give language to help you understand your personal style and implications for your leadership style. Know that no inventory or assessment will tell you who you are, but a certified consultant can help guide and coach you through the discovery process that you validate. For referrals, check with your human resources department or talent management office at work or contact me at www.transportergroup.com.

Reflection/Discussion Questions

1. What mask do you wear when you go to the place in which you lead?

2. Why do you put it on?

3. What is the risk of leading from your authentic self?

4. What is the benefit of leading from your authentic self?

4

Develop an Influence Mindset

*We all have prejudices to dispel: the need to get away from
thinking that 'I' am important and special and 'you' are not,
and the frightened mindset that tells us that certain 'others'
are of no consequence.*

~INGRID NEWKIRK

IN THE INTRODUCTION I described the community of my grow-
ing-up years and used the term ubuntu to describe the interconnectedness of that community and its shaping of my identity for
influence. I've also stated that ubuntu shapes a type of power
that works on behalf of the collective or greater good. Ubuntu
says, "I am because we are." Or put another way, my being, my
existence is interconnected with yours. That interconnectedness
is not only critical to communal identity but to developing an
influence mindset.

Nelson Mandela was one of the world's greatest influencers.
He worked tirelessly to end apartheid in South Africa, was jailed
for most of his adult life, and upon his release became the first
democratically elected President of South Africa.

In his 2013 Ted Talk in tribute to Nelson Mandela, Boyd Varty
recalls that Mandela "said often that the gift of prison was the ability to go within and to think, to create within himself the things
he most wanted for South Africa: peace, reconciliation, harmony.
Through this act of intense open-heartedness, he was to become
the embodiment of what in South Africa we call ubuntu, 'I am;

because of you."[1] At this stage of his life and leadership, Mandela's ubuntu-shaped mindset was such that he could not passively sit by to continue to let racist practices derogate his people and divide his country. Nor would he aggressively overthrow the government and force change. And neither could he undermine or use his influence to manipulate the masses toward his goals. At this stage of his life and leadership, Mandela's mindset was one of influencing for the greater good, with or without formal power.

Gertrude Matshe is a Zimbabwean storyteller and inspirational speaker living in New Zealand. Matshe describes a person with ubuntu as "open and available to others; and is affirming of others. A person with ubuntu has the self-assurance that comes from knowing she belongs to a greater whole and is diminished when others are humiliated."[2] A person with ubuntu affirms others just as valuably as she affirms self. As an undergirding concept to the influence mindset, Matshe reminds us, though articulated by her African culture, living it out is not reserved for Africans. She proclaims, "I am happy to say that I found ubuntu right here in New Zealand. From the day I got off the plane I have met people who extended a helping hand when I needed it. I have met people who showed me the way when I got lost, and who introduced me to other people and so expand my network of business associates and friends."[3] That is the influence mindset in action—people helping people, effecting change for the good and pointing others to a better way.

A mindset is your approach to thinking about people, issues, problems, and situations. Through experience, your cultural upbringing, socialization or social modeling, you develop a mindset that shapes your interactions with others. Some of us have a propensity to work with others for mutual gain, while others of us tend to work against others for personal gain. You have got to make up your mind that you have what it takes to make a difference and influence for good. When it comes to cultivating

1. May, "I Am, Because of You."
2. Matshe, *Born on the Continent*, 20.
3. Ibid, 17.

the influence mindset, you need to know first and foremost what it is not.

The Passive Mindset

Kiana, a young staff member who worked for me not too long ago, had developed a passive mindset and wasn't even aware of it. It didn't take long for me to notice that she rarely gave her opinion, even when asked. When asked for input on the direction our small team should go, she'd reply, "It doesn't matter to me." When deciding on a course of action and I'd ask her for input, she'd often say, "Just tell me what you want me to do." Although Kiana was young and new to the workforce, in order to be successful in the workplace long-term, and make an impact with her creative ideas, she was going to have to shift from her passive mindset.

People with a passive mindset consistently acquiesce to the demands of others because, typically, they assume they have no power or believe they have less power than the others. They do not see their connection to others as an equal connection. They fall into the trap of defining power merely by structural authority and minimize what they bring to any decision-making table, relationship, or position. They tend to change their true perspectives and opinions in order to get along with others. They underestimate their value to the community.

Like Kiana, if you tend to hold on to a passive mindset, you will have to build more confidence and respect in your own power and learn to assert your voice.

The Manipulative Mindset

People who hold to the manipulative mindset believe they have little ability to influence others. Unfortunately, they also believe that others in their system have little or no power to effect change either. These are the people you've encountered who believe they must resort to indirect and underhanded maneuverings. They try to work around the formal power structures yet have not built strong relationships with others. They are a detriment to the community. They come to meetings with hidden agendas. They don't engage in formal meetings but are the first to call the informal meeting after the meeting to complain about the formal structures and other team members. They fail to express ideas and perspectives honestly. They feel stuck and powerless. They fail to speak up and express ideas and opinions forthrightly yet take their complaints and issues "underground." A manipulative mindset creates what some people call "nice nasty" behaviors. I'm sure you can think of people in your organization who operate from this mindset. You do not want to be that person.

The Aggressive Mindset

People who work from an aggressive mindset truly believe in their own power. They believe singularly in their own individualized rights, often to the detriment of others in the community. They have a strong sense of the importance of their own voice and opinions and don't mind forcing them on others. When it comes to influencing, the issue with people with an aggressive mindset is they have little to no respect for the power, voice, or values of others. Theirs is truly an assumption of "power-over." People who operate from an aggressive mindset demand their rights over and above the rights of others. They insist on controlling other people. They push their opinion, agendas, and ideas and proposals on others. Because they assume theirs is the right and only way, they tend to speak in declaratives, dominating conversations and over talking others. This aggressive mindset leads to bullying, which is the antithesis of ubuntu. Though common in popular culture and even in some political arenas, that type of overpowering in most organizations will stall you.

The Influence Mindset

People who have an influence mindset are assertive. They have cultivated a deep respect for the power of the collective and in the spirit of ubuntu, they influence for the greater good and not for self-serving purposes. They believe they have power. They know their voice is important, and they honor their values. They also view the values and power of other people as being just as important as their own.

People who operate from an influence mindset affirm their rights, opinions, and perspectives and they affirm the rights, opinions, and perspectives of others. They refuse to violate or disrespect the rights of others. Because their mindset is anchored in mutuality, they can confidently act in their own best interests and express their perspectives while hearing and respecting the perspectives of others. Effective influencers use assertiveness as a means to influence.

One senior executive told me about an opportunity early in her career that required relocating to another country. Apparently, her manager at the time was not considering her for the role. She challenged her manager and asked, "Why didn't you ask me?" The manager said, "Because I need someone who is more mobile." This manager had made assumptions about her willingness (or unwillingness) to move. Questioning her manager was not an act of disrespect but an affirmation of her belief in her ability to make impact on the whole. She ultimately chose to take the position and moved her entire family to a new country. The manager was trying to protect her, but it was shortsightedness on his part. That woman held an influence mindset, which enabled her to assert herself, speak up, say what she wanted, and not be passed over for what became a career-defining move.

In any given interaction you may adopt an approach to responding or acting upon others that is passive, manipulative, aggressive, or assertive. The key is to examine your assumptions about yourself, others, and the world or culture in which you live and assess your predominant mindset. Following are some tips to help you assess and then move toward an influence mindset.

Think About Your Thinking

In chapter six I review three clusters of power that are operative in organizational life and show how each of us has power. For now let's explore your thinking about power, as an example of the importance of thinking about your thinking.

When faced with a challenge or a conflict, how do you see yourself? Do you believe in your own agency or ability to make choices in your own best interest, or do you depend on and need others to choose for you? Your choices can be unconscious or conscious. These thoughts or assumptions could be undermining your ability to fully engage in and be successful in your context.

Marta was a young undergrad who wanted to become State's Attorney one day. She was concerned about maintaining her values as she moved up the political ladder. She asked me during a lunch-and-learn session for college students, "How will I handle those challenges until I get into power." Marta thought about power (and, therefore, influence) as a commodity that came with the highest positions of authority. She assumed she would have no power. Until Marta shifted her thinking about herself, her purpose, and the perspective on leading, she was setting herself up for acting passively in the face of conflict.

Courtney was the only African American woman on her team. She was a solid performer but saw herself as having no power in her work team or with her manager. Consequently, she often felt as if she had to work around her team to get her work accomplished. She told me that she felt if she spoke up, she would be labeled as the angry black woman. She also believed that if she spoke up or gave feedback on what she saw happening in her team that her assertiveness would run counter to her faith. She thought she was supposed to remain quiet and let God work it out. Courtney's assumptions about using her power had to be explored in light of her spiritual core beliefs, and she had to discover how being assertive did not violate her beliefs. She then had to be coached toward shifting her thinking to valuing her own expert power on the team and not letting stereotypes others held live in her head. I'll say more about how to navigate these types of influence barriers for women in chapter seven.

Emily was a seasoned leader who had a reputation for being outspoken and overbearing with people in her organization. She used what Mary Parker Follett called "power-over" tactics. She said what she wanted to say with little self-monitoring. She had no filters. Emily believed she had earned the right to dictate to others, but instead of garnering influence she was labeled as a bully. If you're like Emily, but want to influence others you work with, you will need to shift your thinking from "my way or the highway" to respecting the right of others to think differently from you.

Create the Space for Dialogue

Too often people try to influence others with an aggressive or power-over approach. They call it influence, but really their aim is to convince the other what is best for the other without really understanding the other. That is not influence.

In any interaction, whether seeking approval for a budget or new project, or persuading people of the community to support an initiative, you have to make space for dialogue. In so doing, you show respect for the other person and, in the spirit of ubuntu, honor your mutual connection. You also have to seek to understand the perspective of the other. Too often people bulldoze one another, ignoring the input of the other because they never fully understood or heard the other. In most work settings, coworkers or colleagues can work together for best solutions without aggressive bullying or self-serving aims.

Dialogue is not just a communication device or type of discourse. It is a defining perspective of influence. Dialogue is a two-way conversation among equals. With dialogue, like ubuntu, equality is not defined by title or rank but by our common humanity. Sometimes our own view of self or others or of the differences in titles prevents us from acting as agents among equals.

I remember early in my career as a consultant, I worked on a corporate organizational effectiveness staff of a Fortune 100 company and often had to make presentations to the CEO's executive committee. One time I had the privilege of reporting our company's employee survey results and improvement strategies to the board of directors.

At the time, civil rights icon Barbara Jordan served as a director on my company's board. I was nervous and awestruck about having to present to her, and I was intimidated by the white male senior leaders who would also be around the table that day. I persevered through the presentation and reported my information, but I left feeling as though I had missed an opportunity to really connect my data on the voice of the employees to that audience. I had given a transactional report, but it could have been a transformational moment, if I had only seen myself as equal in worth to the "big shots" and talked with them and not at them. From that point on, I determined in myself that in any situation in which I needed to influence, I had to see my senior leaders, clients, or other stakeholders as collaborators or co-laborers. And together, through dialogue, we would address the issues and have a transformative conversation.

As influence starts with "I," your mindset is crucial to seeing and acting on your opportunities to influence. In chapter nine, I will offer examples of how the influence mindset helps you recognize everyday opportunities to make a difference.

Put It into Action

Pay attention to your interactions over the next few days. Look for evidence of the following mindsets. In which quadrant do you find most of your actions? As an additional point of feedback, ask a relative, coworker, or colleague to provide feedback on how she or he experiences your interactions. That person's feedback can help you identify your blind spots.

	Aggressive Mindset	Influence Mindset
HIGH	• I demand my rights over and above the rights, opinions, ideas, and perspectives of others • I insist on controlling other people • I push opinions, agendas, ideas, or proposals on others • I speak in declaratives • I dominate conversations • I over talk others • I express inappropriate and hostile emotions	• I affirm my rights, opinions and perspectives as well as affirm the rights, opinions and perspectives of others • I refuse to violate or disrespect the rights of others • I confidently act and express perspectives • I speak clearly and listen intently • I express emotions calmly and appropriately
	Manipulative Mindset	Passive Mindset
LOW	• I resort to indirect and underhanded maneuverings • I maintain hidden agendas • I use backward compliments or humor to conceal real goals and desires • I fail to express ideas and perspectives honestly due to feeling stuck and powerless • I fail to speak up and express ideas and opinions forthrightly yet take complaints and issues "underground"	• I acquiesce to the demands of others out of a belief that I have little or no power • I tend to change my true perspectives and opinions in order to get along with others • I accept being silenced • I tend to use qualifiers and speak less directly • I am reticent to assert myself
	LOW	HIGH

AFFIRMATION of SELF (YOUR OWN POWER, VALUES AND VOICE)

AFFIRMATION of OTHERS
(THEIR POWER, VALUES, AND VOICE)

Where do your actions primarily lie according to your reflections? According to the feedback of others? How do your actions reflect the mindset you most often operate from? What does this say about your influence mindset? If there is a gap, what will you do to change your mindset?

Reflection/Discussion Questions

1. How can the concept of ubuntu help you develop an influence mindset?

2. As a woman, what is your mindset for interacting with and toward other women? Do you tend to have more assertive interactions with women who are like you? What is your mindset toward women who are different from you—who come from a different culture, race, or religion? In what ways are you more overpowering or less powering?

3. What is your mindset in working with and interacting with men? In what ways do you implicitly defer, yielding more power and authority to men?

4. How can you implement dialogue more fully into your leadership?

5

Boost Your Confidence

*If you do not have confidence in yourself, how can you expect
others to have confidence in you?*

~ NORA WU

RECENTLY, WHEN RUNNING A workshop for a corporate women's
leadership group in which four male executive committee members were in attendance, I asked the question, "How many people
have been in a meeting in which you are in the midst of making a
point, and someone interrupts you—just cuts you off and takes the
floor?" The majority of women raised their hands, as did two of
the male executive committee members. I proceeded to provide a
brief communication model distinguishing the difference between
verbal overlaps and interruptions. Verbal overlaps tend to build
on another's ideas and generate and build momentum; while the
interrupt cuts off the first speaker, dissipates energy, and is a com-
petitive, overpowering move—whether intended or not.

At that point, a woman leader recounted, "Those interruptions cause me to lose my voice." And by extension that loss of
voice was closely related to a loss of confidence. It's not unusual for
me to hear comments of that nature. When the aggressive interrupt happens, some women tend to go within and begin mulling
over what happened to silence their voice. Of course, many women
have learned the strategy of not letting the interrupter interrupt,
and they refuse to give up the floor as a momentary crash of words
occurs on the meeting's verbal freeway.

When I asked the men how they felt when the interrupt happened to them, the second most senior man in the room laid back in his chair, chin slightly jutted and declared firmly, "I get pissed." I could see his resolve by his posture: he didn't take interruptions lightly.

What was even more telling in that exchange was what happened after the workshop. One of the male senior execs came to me and said, "I never knew what 'losing one's voice' really meant. I just never realized those interruptions caused some women to shut down." I built upon his point, "Yes, as your colleague stated, for many men, getting interrupted pisses you off, but you raise your voice and take it as a challenge; whereas it shuts many women down."

He never realized the effect such a common verbal pattern had on some women in many workplaces. Could it be that rather than continue to tell women to "raise their voices," we tell men to pipe down and help leaders develop inclusive strategies that work well for all who are on the same team? Could it be that we don't need another book on how women must change to effectively navigate the corporate culture? Could it be that the organizational cultures are changing, and men must also adapt to the changes that come with a more collaborative work environment, which is the hallmark of success for the vast majority in the global workplace? We'll keep working toward these goals!

Still, we must acknowledge the successful influencer is a confident influencer. As surprising as it may sound, successful leaders are judged just as much by their confidence as by their competence. Part of the reason is confidence has two faces—the inward face of your expectations and self-assurance, and the outward face of what you show to the rest of us to assure us of what you have done and can do. So you can be the most competent person in the room, but if you shut down and can't show others your competence, you can't influence them.

One of the things we know about confidence is that some of us are more confident in some situations than others. Each of us can benefit from doing the work that helps us to continue to increase our confidence.

Gender and The Confidence Gap

Much has been written about the gap in the confidence levels between men and women. In actuality, there are two confidence gaps that we must understand.

The first is really more of a question about whether there truly is a gap between men's confidence levels and women's confidence. Renowned journalists Katty Kay and Claire Shipman summarized a number of these studies in their book *The Confidence Code: The Science and Art of Self-Assurance—What Women Should Know.*[1] Studies show women have less confidence than men in some situations such as in salary negotiations, in assessing their ability in analytical reasoning, and even in their beliefs around the percent of capabilities they possess before they will go for a new position.

Some of these differences can be rooted in personal and cultural values, training, socialization, or institutional and organizational barriers. Other studies suggest that measures of confidence are typically anchored in men's behavior. For the most part, many women don't demonstrate confidence in the same way men do; therefore, they should not be measured against this "standard."

I don't want to help you cultivate your confidence so you can influence like a man. I want to help you build your confidence so you can influence like the best *you* that you can be and show it in the way that is most authentic to you. What I have seen is that the confident leader shows the assurance and belief in herself so that others come to trust her actions and experience, and those actions lead to the achievement of desired goals and outcomes.

That means we must take a moment to consider the second type of confidence gap that isn't written about. This confidence gap refers to the space between your current level of confidence and the confidence level you can attain if you let go of fears, inhibitions, or insecurity. This second gap can be great when we are approaching the unknown or unfamiliar such as a new venture or new role. Identifying the situations or issues that tend to diminish your confidence levels is important.

1. Kay and Shipman, *The Confidence Code.*

Confidence Busters and Boosters

What we term as confidence is a complex set of attitudes and behaviors that I liken to a balloon. Factors and situations around us boost our confidence levels much as a balloon is enlarged by blowing air into it. Yet, much like the smallest item can burst a balloon, specific situations or people can bust our confidence and make us tenuous, even apprehensive to move forward or express ourselves. As emerging leaders growing in our influence, we must identify those confidence busters and boosters to help us become more self-aware of circumstances that hold us back or move us forward.

Rosabeth Moss Kanter, author and preeminent Harvard scholar of women's leadership, defines confidence as consisting of "positive expectations for favorable outcomes."[2] I love her definition because it speaks to the inward disposition of confidence. It speaks of the mindset or expectations that each of us can hold that help us move forward expecting a positive outcome. Often a confidence booster helps us to develop an optimistic outlook on our circumstance.

On the other hand, Helene Lerner, in her book *The Confidence Myth*, defines confidence as "the ability to step into uncharted territory and take the next right action, to get comfortable with the uncomfortable."[3] I like her definition too! Learner's description of confidence speaks of the outward display of confidence—one's ability to move forward into the unfamiliar, in spite of the fear, nervousness, or trepidation she feels inside.

As women (and particularly for women of color), many cultural and situational things work to bust our confidence on an almost daily basis. No, we don't let these things stop us. But we must stop sometimes to reflect on the dual assaults of racism and sexism and identify mitigation strategies for our own souls' sake. We have to literally ask ourselves if a certain confidence-busting situation occurs, what are we going to do to handle it wisely and maintain our posture of confidence.

2. Kanter, *Confidence: How Winning and Losing Streaks Begin and End*, 8.

3. Lerner, *The Confidence Myth*, 9.

I have found that there are four levels of confidence busters and four corresponding boosters:

- the societal/cultural level—the memes and popular cultural images and narratives that demean women.

- the organizational level—the practices, policies, and systems of organizational leaders that shape the culture around us.

- the interpersonal level—the people and interactions that affect us.

- the personal level—our own thinking, mindset, emotions.

Building confidence starts within, but it doesn't end there. Each of us must grow in self-awareness to understand not only our own mindsets and thought processes, but also comprehend how institutional practices, cultural memes, and our relationships with others affect our souls. Each of us have to be honest enough to acknowledge whether the place we are in is a place in which the "I" within can flourish and grow, and whether the people with whom we interact on a regular basis help the "I" within to thrive.

I remember my first full-time academic position. I had just completed my doctoral degree when I accepted a tenure-track position in the communication department of a private liberal arts university. My department was diverse, consisting of women and men of various ethnic and cultural backgrounds, sexual orientations, and religious affiliations. During my first semester, an Indian American colleague, Pryia, and I talked quite frequently. She had been on faculty for a few years and was happy to help me navigate the culture of the university, and more specifically the department in which I worked. One day as we were walking, she said, "Jeanne, there are people here who are going to try to make you feel as though you don't belong. But you've got to be certain within yourself that you have earned the right to be here." I initially thought her admonishments had to do with my research area, which was qualitative in nature and focused on African American communities and organizations. At some level, perhaps it was a given that I researched and taught out of my own lived experience, and Pryia was reminding me that not everyone in the institutional power structure would appreciate my work.

As I thought more critically about Pryia's advice, I realized she was stating the fact that the institution I worked in, as prestigious as it was, was not founded or established for people who looked like me or came from my background. And those for whom it was formed acted like gatekeepers; they wanted to maintain their status and privilege and reinforce the perceived outsider status of newcomers such as Pryia and myself, as if they did us a favor by allowing us to work at their university. That constant feeling of being made to question whether one belongs is a confidence buster. This is often done through micro-aggressions or small everyday things, such as questioning your research status; questions about finding "qualified" minority candidates; and even the use of terms such as "minority" or "diverse" candidates. And too many women in organizations and industries everywhere have questioned whether they belong, thus reinforcing the confidence busting cycle. As Pryia said, you've got to know you have earned the right to be where you are by virtue of your skill set, experience, academic training, and perspective.

Now let's delve into the corresponding confidence boosters that can counteract the words and actions used to bust our confidence.

Societal/Cultural Confidence Boosters

Women's Movements

As painful as it was to hear the stories arising out of the #MeToo movement, the tide of women coming forth to tell their truths about sexual abuse and sexual harassment signaled to the world that women were supporting women and men were believing women. The movement buoyed the confidence of other women to come forth with their stories. What started out as a trickle with Tarana Burke[4] first coining the phrase when supporting a young

4. Santiago and Criss, "An Activist, a Little Girl and the Heartbreaking

sexual assault victim (all she could say was "me too") became a national movement. Ms. Burke wanted other women to come forth with their stories of survival and launched the movement. From that trickle in 1996, came a flood in 2017 of #MeToo stories (thanks to modern-day communication vehicles like social media) when celebrities' stories about painful experiences with sexual assault or harassment came to the forefront.[5]

Movements like #MeToo boost the confidence of women to tell our stories, to tell our truths. In fact, Ms. Burke is initiating a new dimension to the movement. She encourages women to not stop at sharing the stories of surviving abuse, but to also tell stories of the process of healing, recovery, and transformation. Those stories boost the confidence of other women to know they can move forward and even thrive after assault.

Brand Marketing Campaigns Highlighting Women's Empowerment

Not so long ago, I facilitated a workshop for women leaders in Lisbon, Portugal. The workshop curriculum included a segment on enhancing our credibility to influence. One of the factors for building confidence that I teach is being comfortable with ourselves: that is, being able to demonstrate ease with our own style, beliefs, ideas, thoughts, and opinions so we convey a level of authenticity to others and for ourselves. I usually talk about being comfortable in one's own skin, among other things.

During that segment of the workshop in Lisbon, one of the women asked if I had seen the video about "curly hair." At the time I had not seen it, and I asked her to describe it for me and her colleagues. She proceeded to describe the story line of the video, in which little girls with curly hair were asked if they liked their hair. None of the girls liked their curly hair. The consumer brand and producer of the short video brought in women with curly hair

---

Origin of 'Me Too."

5. Harris, She Founded Me Too.

to talk to the girls. They even brought in a musical band of curly headed men and women to celebrate curly hair.

I listened intently to the woman's description of the video. As she shared the narrative of the video, I noted her dark curly hair. I then looked around the room at the other twenty-four women and noted that many had curly hair of different colors and lengths. Not wanting to overgeneralize, I did, however, wonder if I was observing the display of a cultural value in which some Portuguese women did not feel compelled to straighten or "tame their hair" for their workplaces, and that was acceptable in their work environments.

A few weeks later I ran a similar workshop in New York City at which mid-level to senior-level women leaders from a number of corporations and government agencies were in attendance. Again, I led a discussion around confidence in women, and a similar discussion ensued during that module. During the break, I overheard two white women with curly hair talking about their choices not to straighten their hair to appear more acceptable at work. One wanted to send a message to her daughter that her hair was beautiful, and the other felt she was more authentically herself when she wore her naturally curly hair. I drew closer and joined them so I could hear more of their perspective.

Those very confident women were making statements about themselves, that their competence was not related to the curl pattern or texture of their hair. In fact, one woman proclaimed she actually felt more creative when she could truly bring her authentic self to work—curly hair and all! It seemed to me what I was hearing from these women was this: being able to bring their true selves to work seemed to be a confidence booster; whereas having to change their appearance to fit into a corporate ideal felt more like a confidence buster.

I decided to watch the video and found it and others like it on YouTube. Some were inspiring and others felt a little contrived. But there were a few that caught my attention. I found myself smiling (that's right, smiling), leaning forward, and jotting down quotes as I watched them. Still a little skeptical, I looked for faces and body sizes, and listened for accents of women from a diverse range of ethnic and cultural groups as I watched those videos. Again, with a few exceptions, they were there. I admit that part of my curiosity about the debate about the effect of wearing one's natural hair in a corporate setting or leadership role may have on how she is perceived was related to a personal decision I had made.

A year or so earlier, I had decided to go natural—to stop chemically straightening my hair and eventually allowing my kinky hair to loc. That was a big step for me as a corporate consultant, especially when some companies had banned or discouraged natural hairstyles such as locs and braids. My own confidence was boosted watching those videos, affirming that my competence as a leadership consultant and coach was not locked into the texture of my hair. I felt I also served as a model for up-and-coming black women professionals who wanted to bring their full selves to work.

So, let me acknowledge that those marketing campaigns have the intent of helping a company sell more products. I get that. Yet there are residual effects of marketing campaigns that can send subtle messages that can either boost women's views of ourselves or bust them.

Those particular marketing campaigns, whether they tout the beauty of curly or kinky hair or say we are more than the size of our jeans, help broaden the standards of acceptability for women. The messaging of such campaigns runs counter to dominant advertising messages. They creatively deal with subject matter from beauty standards to the conversational ritual of saying sorry to gendered double-binds and stereotypes.

And in this media-saturated world, where so much advertising touts implicit (and explicit) standards of beauty and heaps untold pressure on women to measure up to unattainable ideals, I, for one, was pleased to see a number of those marketing campaigns touting a woman's natural beauty. They are not perfect, but many of them make a perfect point giving more and more women the confidence to be themselves both at home and at work.

Though some are becoming more mainstream on network television and streaming services, you can find a great number of them on companies' web-based platforms or YouTube.

Organizational Level Confidence Boosters

Mentoring Programs

Clearly having a Pryia as a colleague, friend, and mentor was a confidence booster for me. The university didn't have a formal mentoring program, but organizations and institutions would bode well to institute formal mentoring programs for new or emerging leaders. Not only do such programs help emerging leaders navigate the culture of their workplace, but, by providing mentors, they also help to mitigate the blows to one's confidence that come from institutional life.

If your organization does not have a formal mentoring program, then seek out a trusted mentor in your organization or in your field. I'll say more about this in chapter eight.

Women's Leadership Training

There is a need for making women's leadership training a part of an organization's diversity and inclusion processes. These programs are crucial for equipping women with requisite leadership skills for advancing. Organizations that are committed to increasing women in leadership must create talent pipelines that identify and develop women leaders, as well as commit to providing access and exposure to emerging women leaders. These development programs are necessary, but as one of my colleagues says, they are not "build-a-better-woman" programs designed to fix women. Instead, they signal to women their importance to the organization, and they create spaces for women to examine the gender realties of their organization and develop strategies and a supportive network.

Women Role Models in Leadership

From the ivory towers of academia to the glassed offices of corporations to the stained-glass sanctuaries of institutions of faith, women are less represented in leadership than they are in the general population or the entry- and mid-level ranks of the same organizations. There are proportionately more women up through middle management ranks than there are in senior leadership, more women in the pews than in the pulpit or denominational hierarchy.

It is critical for women and men coming up the ranks to see women leaders. Women leaders expand our images of what leaders look like. Women leaders give emerging women leaders examples of leadership that "looks like" them. And in many ways, seeing women in senior leadership roles boosts the confidence of women at every level. It says to all of us that if they could make it to the top, then I can make it to places in leadership that I dream of.

Interpersonal Level Confidence Boosters

Amplifiers

The *Washington Post* carried a story about the women staffers in President Barack Obama's administration that has remained with me. One third of President Obama's top aides were women, and they faced what many women in corporations and institutions that are male dominated deal with daily: they felt they had to "elbow their way into important meetings," and "when they got in, their voices were sometimes ignored."[6] However, those women didn't settle for just getting a seat at the table. They adopted a brilliant yet simple meeting strategy that boosted their confidence and started to shift the meeting culture. They labeled their strategy amplification: "When a woman made a key point, other women would repeat it, giving credit to its author. This forced the men in the room

6. Eilperin, "White House Women Want to Be in the Room Where It Happens."

to recognize their contribution—and denied them the chance to claim the idea as their own."[7]

If you find yourself or other women constantly being over talked, connect with other women (and male allies) in your organization or on your team and develop an amplification strategy that can work for everyone.

Collaborators

Collaboration is a confidence booster. Working with another person who sees herself as being on the same team and is committed to achieving the best outcomes boosts the confidence of each woman. Working together without competition allows each person to bring her A game and support the other. Collaborators boost our confidence, especially when everyone involved is assured that the outcome being worked toward is win-win. And when everyone wins, we gain a track record of winning together that creates an expectation for winning in the future.

Personal Level Confidence Boosters

Aligned Purpose

I've already talked about the importance of purpose to influence, but I want to share more insights on purpose as a confidence booster. I remember speaking with Maryam, a mid-level manager, in Dubai. I was leading an Influence workshop there when Maryam sought me out at one of the breaks to ask if she could spend time talking to me after the workshop. I readily agreed. She had come up to me near the end of lunch to let me know she had to go pray but would return to the session. Right then I sensed her faith was a deep value to her.

After the workshop we sat together and she opened the conversation with "I don't know what I want to do next!" She explained to me that she was on the career path into senior leadership but

7. Ibid

was conflicted. "I don't know if I want it, though," Maryam sighed. She then shared how frustrated she was in her company and with senior leaders. She liked working with team members and clients, and she was a strong strategist who led teams that built effective human capital solutions. But Maryam didn't seem fulfilled.

As Maryam continued to talk and share her concerns, I sensed there was something deeper going on within her. A devout Muslim, she was struggling with how her career connected to her reason for being in the world. When she paused, I softly said, "Sounds like you're grappling with your sense of purpose." I could see the tears well up in her eyes. It turns out she was wrestling with how to live out her purpose in that particular workplace. What was most important to her was out of alignment with what was most important to her organizational leader, causing her to question her inclination and desire to continue to move forward in her company.

An executive leader I once interviewed captured Maryam's quandary well. When asked what advice she would give to women about living out their purpose at work, she said, "Focus on finding convergence on what matters most to the organization and to you. If you find it, you find a path upward." When I asked her what if one doesn't find that alignment of purpose, she thought for a moment and responded, "If there isn't one, I suppose you'll look for a path out."

You too will need to gain clarity on your purpose. The clearer you are, the more confident you will become in working out of that purpose. Yes, tough times will still come in any workplace, but deep inside you will be convinced of the reason you do what you do and the importance of your work in the lives of others.

Decisive Action

I checked back with Maryam a year later. She had taken a director role for a different multinational company. She wrote to me the following:

I needed to make a decision about my career, and the next natural step was a senior leader. Since I did not have an opportunity with my old company, I decided to look elsewhere. What was preventing me from taking this next step is my fear and I wasn't sure if this is what I want but I decided I won't really know unless I try. So, here I am.

Clearly, fear is a big confidence buster for many of us. The fear of the unknown, the fear of wondering *Can I really do this?* The fear that comes from wondering *What if I fail?* That fear can make us indecisive. Fear can stall us from moving forward. Fear can cause us to overthink our choices and delay deciding about our options.

After months of toiling over her options, Maryam made a decision. And like Maryam, you will need to make a decision about your future. Making the right decision can help boost your confidence. According to Shipman and Kay, "The ability to make decisions big and small, in a timely fashion, and take responsibility for them, is a critical expression of confidence, and also leadership."

Positive Self-talk

If confidence truly is the expectation of a positive outcome, as I believe it is, then the words you say to yourself are absolutely critical for setting an expectation of success. As one of my friends always used to say, "Words create worlds." Either your words will create a world of success that you will confidently move toward, or they will create a world of doubt that will stall you. In other words, what you say to yourself creates an internal image, or a mental self. NPR's Laura Starecheski spoke with researchers and concluded that "self-talk *is* more than a confidence booster. From a neuroscience perspective, it might be more like internal remodeling."[8] As you change the words you say to yourself from negative to positive, you remodel your own internal imaging that drives your behavior.

So, see yourself succeeding and affirm yourself succeeding. In fact, Ethan Kross, psychologist at the University of Michigan, goes

8. Starechecki, Why Saying Is Believing—The Science of Self-Talk.

a step further and says, use your first name: "_____, you've got this!" In so doing, you begin to think about yourself more objectively, "as though you were another person," and ironically, "it's a lot easier to be kinder to that *other* person."[9]

Be a Confidence Booster to Others

Building your confidence isn't just about you. You can build your confidence by building the confidence of others. Confidence can be contagious.

Each of us can do a number of things to boost the confidence of the women we work with. You can encourage others on your team. You can amplify the voices or ideas of others on the team. You can mentor a new colleague. You can promote or talk up the work of colleagues.

Be Prepared

Without fail you will encounter a situation that will potentially throw you off your game. In some meeting, you will be interrupted in the middle of a point. Your idea may be co-opted in the very meeting you presented it. You've got to decide now how you will handle those situations and maintain your confidence.

9. Ibid

Put It into Action

Over the next few days, pay attention to the situations, people, or things that tend to diminish your confidence. Jot those down in column one. Identify a confidence booster to counteract the things that tend to bust your confidence. Conversely, pay attention to the things that tend to buoy your confidence. Jot those down in column two. When you need a confidence boost, refer to the items you've listed and act upon that item.

	Confidence Busters	Confidence Boosters
Personal		
Interpersonal		
Organizational		
Societal/Cultural		

Reflection/Discussion Questions

1. How does seeing confidence as having two faces make you think about confidence differently?

2. What leadership training does your organization offer for women?

3. Who are the women role models in your organization?

4. With whom in your organization or influence circle can you collaborate on your next project?

5. Who on your team can you work with to amplify each other's voices?

6. For whom can you become a confidence booster?

6

Use Your Power Strategically

*Unless you choose to do great things with it, it makes no difference
how much you are rewarded, or how much power you have.*

~OPRAH WINFREY

I'M NOT MUCH OF a chess player, but it has always struck me as
interesting that the most powerful piece on the chess board is the
queen. Chess players can move the queen in any direction: forward, backward, horizontally, or diagonally. The queen also has
the largest value of all the other pieces. (Of course, players will be
quick to remind me that technically the king has the most value,
because if this piece is captured, the game is over.)

The pawn on the other hand is the least powerful piece. For
me the queen and the pawn are marvelous images of women's influence for too many of us. In our organizations and institutions,
sometimes we've felt more like pawns grinding to get the work
done with little advancement to show for it, when in actuality there
is a powerful queen within us, ready to advance and move. Yes, as
women, we already know we must own our power. The key these
days is being able to use it wisely—not underplaying or overplay-
ing it! In this chapter I want to show you how to use your power
strategically for your own influence and for the greater good.

Power is the ability to get things done. In the organizational
context, power is also the ability to influence and the wise use of
it is foundational to leadership. Power is what enables us to make
things happen. In their classic research, organizational scholars

John French and Bertram Raven developed a typology of five bases of social power in organizations.[1] My extension of their typology comprises nine types of power categorized into three power clusters.

In organizations—be they corporate, church, or community—you need to understand how these power clusters work, self-assess your view and use of power, and then leverage what you have for greater influence. Let's take a moment to define each.

Structural Power

Structural power is the formal power or authority that you have been given by virtue of your role in your organization. According to Dacher Keltner, a social psychologist who studies power, "power is more salient and explicit in . . . organizational charts depicting roles within corporations."[2] Every role has a certain amount of power associated with it in order to make decisions and effect change. Most organizations are structured hierarchically; and therefore, the amount of formal power is directly related to one's level or rank in the organization. The higher you are in the organization's structure, the more formal power you have.

Structural power includes the power you have and wield as a result of the position you hold. As your position expands and increases to direct the tasks of others, you also accrue the power to reward others through the formal performance management system or through the informal system of recognizing achievements. Leaders with structural power have also been known to use coercive power, the power to get results through threat and disapproval.

Unfortunately, too many emerging leaders associate formal power solely with the negative aspects of structural power. In one of my sessions in London, Kathryn, a young emerging leader, reacted strongly to the notion of structural power. In fact, she exclaimed

1. French and Raven, The Bases of Social Power.
2. Keltner, The Power Paradox, 29.

adamantly, "I want to advance in this company, but I don't want that structural power. It all sounds so negative." She worked in a professional services partnership with a collegial environment and I understood her apprehension. Yet, I challenged her with this: "If you are going to advance in this company, you are going to get structural power. You just don't have to use it the way you have seen it used before that has turned you off." Her view of power, like many others, was perhaps formed by more Machiavellian notions of power where power was clearly expressed in terms of "coercion, might and dominance."[3] If maintained, this limited and limiting view of power would keep her from owning the formal power she could earn, and no doubt would hinder her movement in the organization.

Wise is the emerging woman that learns early on the level of formal power that comes with her position, yet not allow herself to be limited or intimidated by formal power. You must understand the decisions that are under your authority to make. You must understand how your role affects other people. Whether you are a senior associate or a senior executive, use the structural power of your position or role as a platform to influence others.

Emerging women leaders must also get comfortable with making the tough decisions that are associated with their role. Some women are apprehensive about making tough decisions that may cause others not to like them. Kitty was a young, emerging leader who took pride in the reputation she had garnered in her organization. People liked her; she was nice. Kitty struggled with making decisions that others in her organization might not like or agree with. She had to learn to gather input, review options with her manager, but in the end, people would respect her more when she made decisions that came with her role and not leave them to others. Every wise and mature woman has had to come to learn that it would be nice if people liked us, but not everyone is going to like us. Instead, we need others to respect us.

Yet making those though decisions does not mean a woman has to make them in brusque, mean ways. Deal with the facts and

3. Keltner, *The Power Paradox*, 18.

issues of the situations and respect the people involved. And by all means, understand how decisions are made in your organization, and know who has the power to make them.

Interpersonal Power

Power is not limited to formal authority. According to Dr. Keltner, "Power is part of every relationship . . . and all relationships prove to be defined by mutual influence."[4] Jenna was a senior executive in a large nonprofit agency who used interpersonal power masterfully. Keep in mind Jenna had the structural power to direct her staff and volunteers by virtue of her role, yet Jenna construed power as a shared resource used for the betterment of her department, the organization in which they served, and the customers they served. She was hired because of her expertise with leadership development. As a former consultant to the agency over the years, Jenna had worked with the staff she had inherited. Finally, theirs was a values-based organization and part of the power base that Jenna stood on to work with and motivate her teams to accomplish great things for the greater good of their organization, clients, and communities they served.

In short, interpersonal power is the power you bring with you into any situation, and through it you interact and effect change in and with others. Jenna used her expert power, or the power that came with her knowledge and proficiency, to lead a staff of other subject matter experts. Interpersonal power also includes the ability to build and maintain trusting relationships, and thus build commitment to mutual goals and values. Jenna often called herself a "player-coach." She was one who led her teams well but would never ask her team to do something she wouldn't do. I saw it time and again with Jenna. During times of crisis, challenges, and deadlines, Jenna would roll up her sleeves and jump in and complete development tasks with her team. Her actions solidified the team's trust of and connection with her.

4. Ibid, 29.

Finally, interpersonal power also includes the ethical power base. Ethical power is the ability to lead and enact change based in sharing, living out, and reinforcing the organization's values. Ethical leaders develop commitment in that their teams and other leaders trust they will do the right thing and that which is in the best interest of the organization, its people, and other stakeholders.

About three quarters of the women I've worked with down through the years are effective because of their use of interpersonal power. Some people argue that we as women develop these skills early on and are socialized to be relational. Believe me, not all women have strong relational skills. But there is something to be said about the gender dynamics of interpersonal power.

Interpersonal power is at the heart of influence. Influence, as we have defined it, is the power to effect change in people, teams, and organizations for the greater good. Another way to put that is influence is the power to get things done without overpowering others. It is through interpersonal power that a great deal of teamwork gets accomplished and tasks and goals are achieved.

In a world in which the need is increasing for relational skills in a variety of organizational and political contexts, those that have developed strong interpersonal power can and must use it to help shape our organizational cultures to reward and expect the strategic use of this type of power.

Women who wield a great deal of interpersonal power tend to take time to invest in relationships even when there is no immediate return. These women build trust and social capital they can draw from down the road, though that was not their initial intent.

In building your interpersonal power, remember to be inclusive. In our increasingly diverse world, you will be a stronger influencer when you have trust with people from a variety of backgrounds. Unfortunately, too many senior leaders rely on a few "go-to" people. This sends a message throughout their organization of favoritism that hurts their influence with the masses.

Because so much of interpersonal power starts with expert power, be willing to speak "expertly" without fear of being labeled as strident or aggressive. Remember, you have expertise that benefits those around you. No one will benefit from it, however, if you keep it to yourself.

Social Power

Social power is a type of power that transcends one-on-one interpersonal relationships. Social power is amassed through networks of relationships. Networks enable you to move beyond your singular department and connect with people across the organization or institution, across the industry, and out into the community or broader marketplace.

Tyra was the quintessential networker. She knew lots of people in her organization, out in the community, and across various industries. She was what Malcolm Gladwell called a connector. The people Tyra connected with didn't become her BFFs, but they were her acquaintances that she had the savvy knack for staying connected to. Gladwell argues, "Acquaintances, in short, represent a source of social power and the more acquaintances you have, the more powerful you are."[5] The impact of their influence is that they "have a special gift for bringing the world together."[6] Connectors help create more cohesiveness among people.

Here's how they do it: they use information power. They share information that gets people to think about issues differently. They use connective power. They connect stakeholders across diverse environments, regions, and industries. And they use brokering power, or they leverage their relationships with significant people on behalf of the causes they advance. People with social power know someone who knows someone who knows someone. In today's social media saturated world, people with social power no longer have to depend on "six degrees of separation," but they can connect to almost anyone else in the world in two or less connections.

5. Gladwell, *The Tipping Point*, 54.
6. Ibid, 38.

Whether you are an emerging leader or an existing leader, an entry-level professional or an executive woman, building your network is key. In my work, I have found networking to be the area that most women need to develop in order to grow in influence. Many women admit to me they don't like to network. Some feel networking is superficial. Many complain they are too busy with the demands of work and family. Still others lament they are just too tired to add one more thing to their already overflowing plates, like going to network events. If you feel this way too, then to build social power you will need to shift your focus from networking to building your network. I'll give you tools for doing this in chapter eight.

In the meantime, here are some strategies for you. As a woman leader, stay abreast of information in your field, organization, or discipline and share it with others. You may not maintain multiple social media accounts or have placement on multiple social media platforms, but it will be helpful to maintain a presence in at least one social media platform. And it doesn't mean you spend all your waking hours tweeting, posting pictures, and sharing articles. Choose one platform and carve out ten minutes or so a day to peruse your timeline or page; connect with those you know and stay abreast of the news related to your industry and that of others in your network.

Take time to build your brand broadly. In one of my client organizations, the culture was such that associates were expected to connect. Mentors would advise their mentees to make sure they have coffee with this person and that person. "Having coffee" was a trope for connecting with significant leaders. It was also a strategy for influence. That organization saw building one's professional network as critical to each person's role as was their position description.

However, just don't have coffee for the sake of having coffee. Prepare for every interaction to be strategic in building your brand with the people with whom you network. Go prepared with questions. Identify ways you can be of mutual service to others in your network.

You may not want to become a person with two degrees of separation in your networks, but you do want to build your social power. Start with and maintain relationships at work, church, or school that grow organically. Again, I will provide tips for developing your social network or support system. Like everything else, it will start with how you see yourself.

Building Your Power Strategy

First, do an internal assessment of your own views of power. To what extent do you define power as merely structural or formal and don't believe you can effect change until you get a powerful title? To what extent do you see power like Jenna, as a shared resource to be used at your current level to help others and the organization become better? Or to what extent do you see power the way Tyra used it, as a base from which to connect people for the greater good? In any event, you must come to see power as the currency of organizational life; own your share of it and use it to influence.

Second, to successfully use power, you must know how it works in your organization. If you are an emerging leader, observe how powerful people operate. Note who is effective—who gets things done without leaving mass casualties behind them. Note how the effective influencers integrate all three clusters of power into their leadership. If you are an existing leader, take note of how you have used power so you can share your wisdom with up-and-coming women leaders.

Third, learn when to use each type of power. In my early career, some women over-relied upon structural power and managed with an iron fist. Many had learned to navigate male-dominated structures without much support and, understandably, wielded power in the best way they could. Learn when to use the formal channels of the organization to gain approval for your work, but use your interpersonal power to gain support for your initiatives and social power to drive change across a broader array of the organization. Commit to using your power for good—the good of others, the good of the organization, the good of the community. A shared power is at the heart of the African concept ubuntu. For when you believe in a shared humanity, you can believe in a shared power.

Finally, understand that powerful women are seen in a certain light. Cultures that privilege male-centric leaders still have trouble accepting powerful women on our own terms. Too often, women still report being labeled in pejorative ways for behaviors that are considered to be strengths in men. For instance, assertiveness in powerful women can be negatively interpreted as aggressiveness, and outspokenness as argumentativeness. I will take up these issues more fully in chapter seven. Just know for now, you must maintain the power to define yourself and not be held captive by other people's stereotypes and tropes.

Can you begin to see yourself as a queen who operates from a cluster of power bases, with many options to move? You have power. You must self-assess and take inventory of your power. Review how you currently use it and how you can strategically use more of your power. Then leverage your strength in order to influence.

Put It into Action

Self-Assessment

Reflect on the way you make things happen in your organization and rate yourself on the following statements.

Type of Power	Definition	Self-assessment (Rate your effectiveness in using this type of power in your organization as low, medium, or high)
Structural Power		
Position Power	the ability to get things done or enact change by using my position, title, office, or rank.	_____
Reward Power	the ability to get things done or enact change by virtue of being able to offer tangible and non-tangible incentives.	_____
Coercive Power	the ability to get things done or enact change by virtue of being able to threaten and disapprove.	_____
Interpersonal Power		
Expert Power	the ability to get things done or enact change by virtue of my knowledge and proficiency.	_____
Relational Power	the ability to get things done or enact change by virtue of being able to relate to others and get others to identify with me.	_____
Ethical Power	the ability to get things done or enact change based on my ability to share, reinforce, and live out the organization's values and be counted on to do the right thing.	_____

Social Power		
Information Power	the ability to get things done or enact change based on my ability to share information that gets people to think about issues differently.	_____
Connective Power	the ability to get things done or enact change by connecting stakeholders and building coalitions of support.	_____
Brokering Power	the ability to get things done or enact change on behalf of another by enlisting the support of individuals and groups.	_____

Reflection/Discussion Questions

1. Prior to reading this chapter, how did you view power? How has that shifted after having read this chapter?

2. Review your self-assessment. With which types of power are you most effective? Explain why this is the case.

3. With which types of power are you least effective? Explain why this is the case.

4. The effective influencer will strategically use all of her sources of power. What can you do differently to use more of your power?

Negotiate Barriers

Always stay true to who you are
—barriers can and will be broken.

~HALIMA ADEN

WE FACE MANY BARRIERS in life. When it comes to influence, I believe the biggest barrier for some of us are things we can't change. "What?" you say. "That doesn't sound like a statement coming from someone with an influence mindset." Bear with me.

The barriers we face as women leaders that provide the greatest challenges to us influencing others are connected to who we are and how we think. The greatest asset you will have to influence others is yourself—that's why influence starts with "I". You are the instrument of influence. Because leadership and much of organizational life is gendered, you will face barriers in the form of stereotypes, and it is crucial for you to learn how to navigate them. You cannot change how others think, but you can change how you respond to their limited thinking.

Unraveling Stereotypes

Sandi was a strong performer who was experiencing challenges at work. An African American woman and the only woman on a team of nearly fifty people, her work was exemplary, as evidenced by her numerous awards. She wrote to me:

> I've received numerous awards, defined my brand, and proven time and again that I can communicate with impact, knock a project out of the park, and think outside the box. Unfortunately, I also feel however, that I have to prove myself every day, not to mention dodging the subtle and not-so-subtle darts thrown at me.

Her concern was that the intention of coworkers who threw those darts was to damage her professional reputation and keep her from progressing at her company. Navigating around the land mines in her company was mentally, emotionally, and spiritually draining for Sandi. A key lesson for Sandi was to learn to navigate around these land mines and optimize her experiences. As one senior executive said recently on a panel, "I can't control what others think of me, but I can control their experience with me."

Sandy was living out a catch-22, or gender double-bind situation, and not experiencing ubuntu in her workplace. When her manager or team challenged her, if she spoke up, they labeled her too sensitive or too defensive. If she didn't speak up, she felt invisible and feared her team and managers would assume she was not adding value and overlook her ability to contribute.

Barriers of bias, be they racial or sexist, not only are energy depleting but can become fear inducing. The first thing you have to do is determine not to let other people's biases stoke your fears and insecurities and diminish your confidence. Do not let other people's biases get into your head. Review your confidence boosters, affirm yourself with positive self-talk, and get a confidence boost from your personal support system. Understand that the biases others hold are not really about you but the result of their distorted mindsets and perspectives.

Your social identity can create barriers to your ability to influence—as others hold stereotypic views about us and we hold stereotypic views about what these identities mean. Sometimes they are called "second-generation gender biases"[1] that shape the minds and practices of leaders that conflict with women seeing themselves as leaders. These messages from existing leaders send conflicting messages to women about whether or not they measure up to the ideal of leader defined in their companies.

Michelle Obama, former First Lady of the United States and best-selling author, describes so vividly how these stereotypes work to trap us.

> I was female, black, and strong, which to certain people . . . translated only to "angry." It was another damaging cliché, one that's been forever used to sweep minority women to the perimeter of every room, an unconscious signal not to listen to what we've got to say. I was now starting to actually feel a bit angry, which then made me feel worse, as if I were fulfilling some prophecy laid out for me by the haters, as if I'd given in. It's remarkable how a stereotype functions as an actual trap. How many "angry black women" have been caught in the circular logic of that phrase? When you aren't being listened to, why wouldn't you get louder? If you're written off as angry or emotional, doesn't that just cause more of the same?[2]

These traps are all too pervasive in organizational life. One of the first things we have to insist on in all of our companies is the development of diversity and inclusion processes that help current leaders recognize their own biases and develop remedies for bias that are more systemic. Diversity and inclusion processes aimed at shifting how we define leadership are also helpful for positioning women to see themselves as leaders and providing strategies for getting un-trapped from the implicit gender biases of others.

The More Things Change

Whether we like it or not, implicit notions of leadership and leading are still pretty male-oriented. Nearly twenty years ago, Catalyst

1. Ibarra, Ely, and Kolb, *Women Rising*, 2013.
2. Obama, *Becoming*, 265.

Inc., a nonprofit consulting group specializing in gender issues, conducted a study revealing the gender stereotypes embedded in the perceptions of senior leaders. Catalyst published a report entitled *Women "Take Care" and Men "Take Charge:" Stereotypes of U.S. Business Leaders Exposed*.[3] The report revealed that top corporate leaders thought women were better at the more relational dimensions of leadership and men the more strategic dimensions of leadership. Women were pegged as the nurturing, caring leaders but were seen as not able take charge and, well, lead. Due to this and similar gender stereotypes, women's advancement into more senior levels of leadership has been hindered. Things haven't changed much.

These stereotypes still play out in a number of ways that, in very subtle ways, hinder some of us from really seeing ourselves as leaders. For instance:

- Women are expected to be more nurturing; yet when we are, we get labeled as the "office mother." We are considered to be very caring but not ready for "leadership," however leadership is defined in your company or institution.

- Women are often expected to take on the scribe or administrative roles on task forces and committees, but men are rarely asked to do the same.

- Women who do the same work as men are given different titles. Women are also often paid less or nothing compared to men in comparable roles or capacities.

As an influencer, don't be trapped by gender stereotypes. If left unchecked, they will restrict the use of your gifts and place you into your designated boxes regardless of your interests, expertise, or potential. As a woman leader, you will likely experience gender stereotypes or prejudice at some point. As one woman executive shared with me, "You can't focus on the barriers; they are everywhere." You have to set your goals, find support, and move forward. If you find yourself on the receiving end of a stereotype as a

3. Catalyst, "Women 'Take Care' and Men 'Take Charge.'"

woman, here are some things you can do to address that bias and shift your own thinking, as well as that of others.

Get Out of the Either-Or Box

Effective leadership consists of two dimensions: relational and strategic. The best leaders are both relational and strategic, not either one or the other. Consequently, influencers are also both relational and strategic. Some people will try to box you into the relational side of the leadership equation because you are a woman. Don't let others box you into one style that fits their view of influence and not your own style. People who lead with an influence mindset look at the big picture as it relates to the community or all involved and at the same time care for the community or groups they lead. One senior executive leader with such an influence mindset says she "takes charge with care."

Keep Calm and Carry On

Stereotypes are rooted in cultural bias. While a stereotype may be directed at you, it's not about you, per se. Prejudice against women leaders is actually about the other person buying into a system of conscious and unconscious inequity based on gender. Do not internalize their bias whenever possible. It's natural to be hurt and angry when someone subjects you to a stereotype, and his or her prejudice needs to be addressed. But it's also important to think reflectively and to choose your internal response wisely.

Recognize Code Words

In every culture there are codes or shortcuts for shared meaning. In some organizations and communities, these codes or words are so ingrained in the culture that people in the culture no longer question their meaning. As new members enter into a culture or system, they have to ask questions about the codes. So too must women listen for and then question code words that reveal gender stereotypes.

In one organization, men who were senior leaders tended to compliment hard-working women, noting they were "grinders," or they could really "grind out the work." Senior women leaders noted that on the surface this sounded like a commendation to the hard work ethic of junior women in the organization, but behind the words was the belief that "though these women were hard working, they were seen as doers, but not as being strategic enough for leadership."

One of my clients heard that leaders thought she had "sharp elbows." The metaphor points to the notion of people pushing themselves through a crowd. For me this code evoked images of aggressive play on the basketball court. In a not-so-subtle way, that talented woman was being told she was seen as aggressive and perhaps self-serving.

Speak Up

Becca Lais describes hearing code words applied to her school leader that she described as a "phenomenal black female principal . . . who worked in a white male/white female environment."

"Aggressive, passionate, strong willed, too difficult to work with, and pushy."

Becca wondered if her principal would have received such labeling had she been white. Becca didn't stop at wondering—she spoke up. She wrote an article about unravelling these stereotypes of black women leaders to inform and hopefully transform leaders in her field.[4]

You can speak up in your own way. First you can discuss the dynamics with decision makers, coaches, or mentors for tips on addressing their use in your organization. By asking about the selective and biased use of certain code words, you are also raising

4. Lais, "The Purposeful Silencing of Black Women."

your leaders' awareness around the meaning and impact of such labels on valued existing and emerging leaders.

Ask Powerful Questions

You will have to ask questions and discern the underlying roots of bias against women leaders. Sexism and patriarchal roots run deep in some philosophical and theological perspectives and traditions. Asking questions will encourage leaders and coworkers who have limited ideas about gender roles to examine their assumptions.

Millie, a mid-level seasoned leader in a male-dominated equipment company told me about a time she attended an assertiveness training seminar. At the end of the year, when it was time to list all of her accomplishments for her performance review, Millie's list included the seminar she had attended among her achievements.

When she sat down with her manager, a seasoned male leader, he scanned her list with his pointer finger and abruptly stopped when he got to the line where the seminar was listed. He quite forcefully exclaimed to her, "See, that's what I'm talking about. You of all people did not need to take a course on aggressiveness."

Millie, somewhat perplexed, maintain her calm and directly asked her manager, "Excuse me? What are you talking about?"

He boisterously charged again, pointing adamantly at the document: "You didn't need to take a course on aggressiveness."

Finally, Millie looked at him and then back to the paper and asked, "Do you mean this course here: Assertiveness Training?" Quite shamefacedly, her manager had to apologize. But his reaction let Millie know that her manager interpreted her actions through such a lens. So strong were his views of strong women that he read a-s-s-e-r-t-i-v-e-n-e-s-s as aggressiveness!

Resist getting defensive and ask questions. Ask for clarity. Ask rhetorically. Ask so that the other person has to think about what was said and what their words truly mean.

Speak to Other Leaders

When you encounter bias—whether that be due to gender, race, class, ability, or something else—speak with a trusted advisor, mentor, or pastor about the patterns you've observed. Discuss what you believe those patterns indicate, their impact on you and other women, and even their consequences for men. Find out what policies exist to protect and empower women and ask your organization to be transparent about them.

Here are a couple of examples of questions you might ask: What practices and policies are in place to ensure women's voices are heard equally in meetings? How are gender issues handled in learning curriculum and sessions?

Join or Create Safe Spaces

From years of leading women's trainings in corporate settings, I have learned that women who live, work, and worship in male-dominated systems and spaces need safe places to both tell our truths and develop support strategies for addressing sexism. In the next chapter, I share keys to developing your support systems.

As I mentioned earlier, join your company's women's affinity group. Some companies provide these business or employee resource groups as a means for creating the spaces for all employees to learn about gender issues in the organization, to network, and to hear from guest speakers and senior leaders.

If your company doesn't have a women's affinity group, then collaborate with other women leaders to advocate for creating one. I am working with a couple of women who influenced their company to create a "women in technology" group to support the advancement of women in their tech company. They initiated programs to support the development of women, as well as their own development. What started out as influencing for programs turned into a systemic change for that company led by those two women. They internalized a leader identity and came to see that they could bring about real change for the good of all.

As a leader (or an emerging leader) you may face many barriers, but the stereotypic gender barriers are the ones that can wreak the most havoc to your influence. Why? Because those are the ones that, when left unchecked, can creep in and take residence in your head and crush your confidence. Or worse, they can cause you to internalize the stereotype and thwart your belief in yourself.

Put It into Action

1. Make a list of the code words and stereotypic actions you have experienced in your place of work, worship, or community. Develop a set of questions to use the next time you hear those words applied to yourself or another woman.

2. Research your organization's gender equity policies and programs. If there are none, approach human resources or your leader to initiate such programs and policies.

Reflection/Discussion Questions

1. Think of a time when you were on the receiving end of another person's bias or stereotype. How did it make you feel? What did you do as a result?

2. How would you handle that same situation today after having read this chapter?

3. How would you encourage or coach other women in your organization to handle such barriers?

8

Develop Your Support System

The connections in and between women are the most feared, the most problematic, and the most potentially transforming force on the planet.

~ADRIENNE RICH

NOT TOO LONG AGO, my company secured a large training contract that included facilitating leadership development sessions globally. There was a possibility that we would facilitate a few sessions in Latin America, and I reached out to my network to identify a Latina who could partner with me to provide that training.

I called Arbin, one of my former university students who had become a leader in a large consulting firm, and asked him for suggestions. He recommended I talk to Kristine. Kristine was a delight to talk with, and we connected right away. Kristine's work entailed coaching high potential leaders from under-represented groups. Her energy and commitment to her Latina culture, as well as her own sense of identity, struck me as so powerful. We both were committed to developing women leaders, and though we didn't get to work together on that engagement, we connected on social media and have stayed in touch for the last couple of years.

Whether you call it your network or your circle of connections, having a strong set of personal and professional relationships has been proven to be the most effective way to grow your influence. Whether your goal is to find a job; secure financing for new business start-ups; expand your customer base; secure recommendations for travel, facilities and venues; or for building a set of associations for professional support and resources, having a diverse and strong network is critical to success or finding the right resource. People tend to tell others in their network about poor customer service; you need to know people who know people. People tend to look to people in their networks for suggestions when hiring and placing new employees. And in this social media-saturated world, many of us belong to multiple networks in which we share and give support, encouragement, advice, and wisdom.

However, many women, particularly from cultural groups who value developing strong ties and connections with others via the family and community, don't like what they consider to be the superficial nature of networking. These cultural groups have values around connecting authentically, and the best connections are done through building relationships of significance. Kristine, for instance, shared that the messages she and other Latinas of her generation received included *"No te eches flores"* (a caution to those who thought a little too highly of themselves). According to this view, a Latina reaching out to other professionals to share her accomplishments could be seen as self-promoting.

Further, Kristine even recalled hearing her dad telling her, "They don't pay you to socialize with your coworkers." The thought was that networking was seen as something not directly related to the day-to-day job and, therefore, not of value.

For some, getting comfortable with building a network or support system requires a shift in mindset from thinking about the activity of networking as merely going to happy hours, networking events, and the like, to the process of building your support system with purposeful connections in order to accomplish goals of mutual benefit. In these cases, authenticity in relationship building is key. A successful consultant and coach, Kristine shared her experience: "I began thinking of networking as two of us finding out how we can help one another." For her it's meeting and connecting with people with whom she has common goals in order for them together to help others. It allows her to network and be authentic to who she is.

Like the concept of ubuntu, whether we recognize it or not, we are connected; and those connections amplify our ability to help and serve others. Operating from ubuntu, you cannot network in mechanistic, utilitarian, self-serving ways—and you don't have to. You can build your circle of support in organic ways that are more authentic to you.

Personal Support

I have a strong circle of connections. We are all pretty high achieving, goal-oriented women and men. We support each other in our respective businesses. We've cried with each other. We pray for each other. We give each other tough feedback. We work hard. We have fun. We support each other.

When my consulting business began to grow, and I needed more structure, I called Helen. Helen is a former executive for a telecommunications company and has successfully run multiple businesses. Helen has established and built up a strong infrastructure of support professionals who support her businesses. Helen recommended a business strategist that restructured my business and provided financial advice.

Then, as I needed to add contract consultants, again, the first place I looked was to my circle of connections. Colette, for instance, was a friend of some twenty years. We had met while both serving on a ministry team at our church. We quickly found out we were both organizational development consultants who happened to work in different business units of the same company! My department had an opening for which I recommended Colette. She applied, went through the interview process, and was ultimately hired. I left that particular company to go to a professional services consulting firm a few months after Colette joined the team. But she and I stayed in touch down through the years, supporting each other personally and professionally.

My support circle also includes men who have been allies for women well before the term became popular. Another person I partnered with in business was my friend Leland. Leland and I met during our stint at a professional services firm. We were often paired on diversity training assignments. As a European American man and an African American woman working together, we provided unique perspectives on diversity. When we both left the firm to branch out on our own in our respective companies, we often partnered together. And our friendship grew. I read scripture at his wedding, and he attended mine a few years later. To this day we can call on each other for support.

In building your circle of connections, look to friends who support you and be willing to get out of your comfort zone and invite women and men into your circle who may be racially, ethnically, or culturally different from you. Diverse circles or networks expand our platform for influence as they connect us to people our "just like me"[1] networks don't or can't.

Operational Support

Nancy was a seasoned executive who I had the great fortune of interviewing for one of my company's projects. I asked her what contributed most to her successful advancement. Without hesitating, she replied, "I had trusted colleagues and peers who knew what I was going through, allowing me to vent with advice and guidance when I was feeling stuck."

Herminia Ibarra, professor and noted researcher on gender and networks, defines this circle of colleagues that we connect with to get our work done and to work through issues at work as our "operational network."[2] She goes on to say, "Networks are what allow you to generate new ideas, to get the information and support that you need and to expand your influence."[3] Look around you. Who are the people you work with that you can collaborate with, can work through ideas with? Who are the people on your team that you have come to rely on and they on you?

1. Magliozzi, "Building Effective Networks."
2. Ibarra, *Building Effective Networks*
3. ibid

Strategic Support

Ibarra defines strategic networks as "relationships that provide new information, resources and opportunities for advancement." She argues that "strategic networks are of the utmost importance, yet are the hardest type to cultivate" for all professionals but especially for women.[4] Cultivating strong strategic support is essential to advancing your ideas and projects. Strong strategic support helps you gain access to decision makers, because undoubtedly, networks are made up of people who know people who know people.

In most organizations, men are the senior leaders and decision makers. Ibarra reminds us that "when women do manage to gain an audience with senior male executives, their ability to form meaningful relationships may be hindered by gender biases."[5]

Kelly works for a consumer goods company and recently attended her company's townhall. In these townhalls the CEO and other senior leaders speak to the employees giving updates on the company and providing a point of connection for the employees to senior leaders. At that particular townhall, the CEO shared a story about a golfing trip with a few other business CEOs. To his dismay, each of the other CEOs reported not being willing to mentor women for fear of being falsely accused or for backlash from the #MeToo movement. Not only is this perspective shortsighted and wrong, but it is also unfortunate for the women of these companies. And chances are they don't even know of the hidden biases held by their top leaders.

On the other hand, Kelly's CEO affirmed his and the company's commitment to gender equality. Kelly's CEO is a strong advocate for equality and a male ally. In organizations whose senior leadership is still male-dominated—many corporations and faith institutions—cultivating and having male allies is helpful and critical to the development of women leaders.

4. ibid
5. ibid

Male Allies Supporting Women

One of my clients has a strong women's affinity group that has been active for nearly fifteen years. Recently, a male executive agreed to serve as the executive sponsor of this affinity group. He is an African American man who is a strong ally of women in the workplace. I interviewed him not too long ago. During that interview, he said something that stuck with me. "Although I had maleness in common with senior leaders of our company, I was still an outsider as a black man. I, too, have had to develop strategies to gain access." He now uses his influence to coach, develop, support, and aid women who may be or feel like outsiders to help them gain access to senior decision makers. In short, male allies are willing to advocate and support women and organizational initiatives aimed at developing and advancing women.

No doubt, there are men in your organization who are open to serving as allies to you and other women. Pay attention to the men who gain a reputation for challenging the status quo and advancing organizational and structural initiatives that support and bring out the best in all employees, including women.

Women Supporting Women

Women are changing the landscape of organizations as more women have advanced the leadership ladder. Connie was elevated to executive vice president after years of stellar organizational and personal performance. One of the first things she did in her executive committee role was create "women's co-mentoring circles." As a woman who lives by ubuntu, Connie knew she had her hard-won success due to her stellar work but also to the support she had been given by sponsors, mentors, allies, and her community. Connie created the co-mentoring circles as a formal initiative within her company to groom women for advancing into leadership. Hailing from the black women's club movement, Connie's motto is *Lift as you climb, this is a not a solitary pursuit.*

I met Nicole at a seminar I was running in Kansas City. She came up to me during the networking time and introduced herself. She was a manager of organizational development for a local company and a thirty-something-year-old mother of a three-year-old. She was contemplating launching her own consulting business as a means for allowing her and her husband to manage both their careers and their family. Nicole asked me if I could mentor her as well as keep her in mind for any projects she could work on. I asked her to send me her resume and I'd see where there was a potential fit. Nicole had great experience and a strong educational background in organizational and leadership development. I was happy to both mentor her in launching her business and hire her as a consultant.

In workshops that I run for existing and emerging women leaders, inevitably someone will tell a story about a senior woman who won't support other women. Or someone will share how they receive the most resistance from other women in their organization.

I've long believed that when it occurs, competition and lack of support among women come from those hierarchical structures that were not created for us and up until recently, didn't include us. Even though the percentages are increasing, women still hold a smaller proportion of leadership positions in most organizations. As Susan Shapiro Barash, author of *Tripping the Prom Queen: The Truth about Women and Rivalry*, puts it: "On some level, we know we haven't yet arrived at full equality."[6] In other words, the limited number of opportunities for women into senior leadership can be likened to a limited slice of the pie. "When you compete for a limited slice of the pie, you naturally tend to focus all your anger on your rivals."[7] Competing with other women for a slice of the pie, holding other women to higher standards, or failing to support up-and-coming women are behaviors that emerge from structures that create zero-sum games for women—making any one woman

6. Barash, *Tripping the Prom Queen*, 42.
7. Ibid, p. 42.

feel that in order for her to win, another woman has to lose because there is only enough room for a few of us.

That cannot continue to be the norm. Shapiro Barash adamantly declares that we must "focus not on the contest for limited goods but on the larger goal: making more good things available to everyone."[8] So yes, we must support each other and together work to change the nature and assumptions of the game. You can support other up-and-coming women by becoming a mentor to a new colleague. Invite a colleague to coffee or lunch. Support each other in meetings. And, by all means, speak up when one of us is being disparaged.

Cultivate Your Circle

Here are a few roles or types of people that you will want to consider as you look at strengthening your network or circle of support.

Coaches. A coach is a professional who helps other professionals set and maintain goals, identify barriers, and move toward their envisioned success. Many companies provide executive coaches for their senior leaders. Others reserve coaches for leaders who have performance issues. In some of those companies, working with a coach is not seen as a positive thing. Dana was a mid-level professional who was very active in her company's women's affinity group. She had a desire to advance into more senior levels of leadership and wanted a coach to help her work through issues that could help her advance. However, she would not have been on the list for her company to provide her with a coach. So, Dana shared with me, "I decided to invest in myself!" She courageously sought out and is working with a coach in order to optimize her own success. There are many options these days, from executive coaches, to career coaches, to life coaches. Do your homework: ask your personal support circle for recommendations or google articles on what to look for in a coach.

8. Ibid, p. 42.

Connectors. A connector is a person who knows many people in various businesses, professions, and industries. They have the distinct ability to socialize in and span many different worlds. They are gifted at making acquaintances and friends and staying linked to them, albeit loosely and casually. Connectors know people who know people. Connectors are masters of the multitude of acquaintances.

Sponsors. A sponsor is a member of the established power structure, an officer or senior leader who has already attained the highest level of leadership. Sponsors provide opportunities and access for emerging leaders. However, a person coming up the ranks does not seek out a sponsor; instead, an up-and-coming leader must be identified and invited by the sponsor. The sponsor, because of his or her senior standing and strategic vantage point in the organization, is in a position to provide visibility to the work of an up-and-coming leader, provide budget support for an up-and-coming leader's projects, and can speak about this person and her successes and qualities to other executives.

Mentors. A mentor is a trusted person who provides counsel and advice concerning one's career. The mentor typically has more experience and provides advice based on his or her experiences and successes in navigating the organization, system, or discipline in question. Rarely does a professional woman these days have just one mentor. In fact, due to the complexity of our leadership paths, our professional disciplines and careers, rarely does one person have the experience and wisdom to mentor another person in all aspects of his or her career. Instead, many seasoned women advise junior women to seek out at least two mentors—one who has experience navigating the current place of work or business and a mentor who has experience in the profession or chosen discipline.

Mentees. On the flip side women at any level of leadership are in position to mentor more junior colleagues. By mentoring others, not only is a leader investing in emerging talent, but she is also helping to inculcate successful leadership values in junior colleagues and developing "bench strength." In many cases, more junior colleagues can also mentor more senior colleagues by giving them insights into generational trends and differences. Obviously, the number of people a leader mentors must be balanced by time constraints and other responsibilities, but mentees can be valuable resources in an influencer's infrastructure of support.

Promoters. A promoter is a person who endorses you and your track record behind the scenes or in the informal network. Some argue that a leader must always be able to speak of his or her competence, thus promoting herself. Yet the reality is that when a leader excels at what she does, and her competence becomes known, people within the organization will promote or endorse her work. Of course, it helps to strategically share your accomplishments with would-be promoters. So, select your promoters wisely, choosing people who can speak to your accomplishments; and spend some time apprising these promoters of your goals, past experiences, and accomplishments so they can speak cogently about you and your accomplishments.

Advisors. All professional women need wise people to whom they can turn for discreet advice. Carla Harris, a managing director of a Wall Street investment firm, defines an advisor as "someone who can answer your discreet career questions, those that may be isolated questions pertaining to your career but are not necessarily in the context of your broader career goals."[9]

Collaborators. These are colleagues who hold similar roles to you but in a different part of the business or agency. These are people in your industry or field who work on similar problems as you do. Collaborators are useful in your network in that they provide operational support and can help you think through projects, programs, and problems that you both face in your line of work. For instance, project managers have been known to collaborate with other project managers.

9. Harris, *Expect to Win*, 2009.

Organizations to Keep in Mind

Women's Affinity Groups.

The twenty-first century has become the century of social networking. Technology has facilitated the proliferation of online social networking, and perhaps spawned the resurgence of face-to-face networking in industry and professional associations. More and more women are flocking to their company's women's affinity groups. These groups serve as a safe place and mechanism for women to connect, learn, grow, and support each other. Members of these groups provide support and information to each other, and in some companies, senior leaders tap into the members of these affinity groups in order to gain business insight into specific demographic markets. Networking opportunities, including conferences and association meetings, are great for professional development and building business contacts. Check out your company's women's affinity group as a first start for building your support system.

Community Service.

Volunteering and serving in nonprofit organizations are great ways to give back to the communities in which you live and work, as well as to build upon your support network. Organizations such as museums, community theaters, and faith-based institutions need time, energy, and money. When you give, keep in mind there are other like-minded people who also give of their time, talent, and treasure to these organizations, and these organizations are sources of connections for all of you.

Building your network in traditional ways can be time consuming, especially for women. Here are some closing tips:

- Form connections organically and diversely. Connect with people in the places you frequent—work, church, the gym, and so on.

- Make building connections a part of your job. Reach out to colleagues or collaborators to brainstorm ideas for new projects. Ask colleagues for suggestions on senior leaders who need to know about projects you are working on.

- Talk to your manager about your career goals and seek out her recommendations for connections that would be most salient to what you are working on.

- Be open to provide information or perspective when others reach out to you.

As you look at examining and strengthening your support system, consider whether or not you are making real connections. Always think about who you are meeting with and why. Getting to meet with people and connect with people you have common interests with will strengthen your influence.

Put It into Action

Who Is in Your Network?

Take a moment to think about your support system. List the top ten people who are a crucial part of your network—these would be people who provide personal, operational, or strategic support to your leadership. What purpose do they serve in your network?

Name	Role/Organization	Why are they in your network? What is the purpose or role they serve in your network?
1.		
2.		
3.		
4.		
5.		
6.		
7.		
8.		
9.		
10.		

Analyzing Your Network of Connections

Instructions:

Review the list of the top ten people who are a crucial part of your network. Given the network roles we reviewed on the previous pages, identify the various roles people in your network play by placing their names in the appropriate circle. Notice there is an additional circle for you to add an additional role that you deem important to your network.

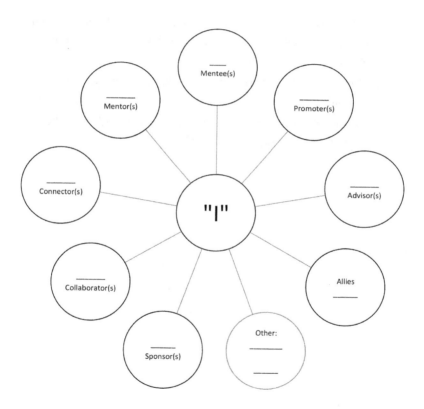

Reflection/ Discussion Questions

Take a moment to review your network diagram. What themes do you see?

1. How diverse is your network?

2. What gaps do you see in your network?

3. Who in your organization would be helpful to your career goals but are not in your network? Who in your network can introduce you to these people?

4. Who have you been advised to connect with? What potential role could they play in your network? What is your strategy for connecting with them?

5. How do you make sure your networking relationships are not one-sided?

6. As a result of this chapter, what action step will you take to strengthen your support system?

9

Recognize Everyday
Opportunities to Influence

*There's no greater gift than thinking that you had
some impact on the world, for the better.*

~GLORIA STEINEM

PRIOR TO OUR MARRIAGE, my husband was a meat and potatoes
guy. I had stopped eating red meat and pork over thirty years ago.
As two working professionals, we share the household duties, including the cooking. Seated at dinner one evening eighteen months
after having said, "I do," my husband took note of the dinner I had
prepared for the two of us. That evening, he jokingly remarked, "I
can't believe how much my diet has changed since I married you.
I prepare and eat more fish, vegetables and healthy grains, and less
salt. When we were dating, you said you wouldn't impose your
eating habits upon me. So, what happened?"

Without missing a beat, I replied, "I said I wouldn't impose
my eating habits upon you, but I never said I wouldn't influence
you!" What started in jest actually revealed the positive impact that
our daily interactions and choices can have on the people around
us. Unfortunately, too many people in workplaces overlook those
opportunities to positively connect with others and never grow
their influence. Too many people don't recognize or see where they
can influence even in small ways.

Perceptual Lenses

The influence mindset can shape how you see or perceive your world. The influence mindset can help you recognize opportunities for you to have positive impact. It serves as a set of lenses that enable you to select information from your environment, organize it to make sense of it, interpret it, and then act. When you believe you can make a difference, that you have a purpose to make a difference, and are even called to make a difference, you start seeing and recognizing opportunities to use your influence to make that difference.

Ayden was a senior leader of a technology organization that I had the opportunity to interview about his perspectives on developing women for more senior leadership positions. At one point I asked him, "What are the barriers to advancement that women in your organization face?" He responded pretty quickly with "I don't know of any barriers women in our organization face!" Then, as if really hearing himself, he more reflectively continued, "And if I don't know that, then perhaps I am the barrier." Wow! Talk about an insight. The underlying philosophy to the influence mindset requires a conscious shift in how we think of ourselves and also how we think about others.

Carly Robb, writer for the *Medium*, puts it this way: "As individuals, we are equipped with particular talents and strengths. Though it is natural for us to want to use these for our own self-progression and success, if we use these qualities to better our community, we reap both personal and societal benefits. We do not have to sacrifice personal success for the community's success, but we must strike a balance between the two."[1]

You have gifts to offer to your organization, community, or institution that are unique to you. In so offering them, you not only enrich the collective, but you enrich yourself. As Nelson Mandela said, "Ubuntu does not mean that people should not enrich themselves. Therefore, the question is *Are you going to do so in order to enable the community around you to be able to improve?* Influence

1. Robb, Ubuntu: I Am Because You Are.

starts with the "I" within you and emanates out into the organization, community, or collective. Like Ayden, you have got to see or reflect on those situations in which you can have an impact even in small ways.

For instance, Sandra was a Puerto Rican consultant that I worked with many years ago. Her skin tone was very light, and she had taken the Anglo last name of her husband, so she was a Latina that many European Americans identified as "one of their own." Consequently, their perception of her was based on her skin tone and last name; they organized that information into their mental schema, interpreted her as white, and said things to her they might not necessarily say to someone who was more visibly Latina, or a woman of color. These types of awkward conversations more often than not happened with colleagues or leaders who did not know Sandra well.

Sandra shared one such incident with me about being among a group of leaders discussing diversity and their resistance to having to adapt to all these "new people" they were being forced to bring into the workforce and advance into leadership. At that moment Sandra had a choice: remain quiet and let the conversation continue or speak up and address the leaders about their limited thinking. She chose to speak up, both revealing her own identity and commitment to diversity. She didn't stop there. Sandra turned that incident into a teachable moment to explore those leaders' resistance to the company's diversity and inclusion programs and explore possibilities that were in the best interest of the company and their respective organizations.

Sandra risked her comfortable position with those leaders to challenge the mindsets of decision makers and shapers of her workplace culture. As those leaders and decision makers changed their perspective, they then could change the policies and practices that could create a more inclusive culture for all.

Each day you are faced with some choice of whether or not to speak up, speak out, and help someone see things in a new light. Here are some things you can start with now.

Your Morning Greeting

Daphne, a dear friend, told me of a time she was frustrated in a particular workplace. "Dr. J (as she calls me), my manager doesn't even speak to me. Literally, he has to walk by my desk to get to his office in the morning and he doesn't speak." He gave no greeting, no good morning, no hello. I asked her if she spoke to him. She said she did, but even then there were times he did not return her greeting. He just plowed forward rushing to his office.

Perhaps Daphne's manager was stressed, pressed, and preoccupied. But speaking to colleagues in the morning acknowledges them, and as Mandela says, recognizes their humanity. To not speak signals to that colleague she is not important to you and she only exists in your world to get things done for you.

Recognize your power to influence your culture by greeting your colleagues with a genuine hello and a smile. You communicate to them "I see you."

Carve Out Your Niche

I interviewed a male ally for a corporate women's network event. This ally was a senior executive who, as an African American man, had influenced his way into senior leadership echelons. He was not automatically invited in. Early in his career, he said he began to identify and take responsibility for the tasks and projects that none of his colleagues wanted. Those tasks and projects were always in line with his strengths and gifts. He carved out his niche. In so doing, he established credibility and a reputation for excellence. He became a go-to person that others could rely on, and he built an organization around the expertise that he cultivated. His influence grew.

There is no greater joy in influencing and cultivating growth in others and in the organization than to be able to do so from a set of gifts and skills about which you are passionate. Carve out your niche based on the needs of the organization and the skill, abilities, gifts, and experiences that are uniquely yours.

Explore Creative Avenues for Pursuing Your Passion

At the heart of my influence is that I am a teacher. I cannot *not* teach—whether in the university classroom, a corporate learning program, or a church conference. My classroom is now mobile as I "teach" leaders in adult professional settings and not solely in traditional college classrooms. Yet I have been open to other venues for "teaching." For instance, some time ago, I was asked to bring mini lessons to share with a radio audience. For five years or so, I "taught" on Chicago radio inspirational daily lessons. I still hear from people who remember those lessons. That platform for influence impacted the broader community.

Look for the Intersection of Your Passion and the Needs of Others

Frederick Buechner in his groundbreaking glossary of terms for the human spirit defines vocation as the "place where your deep gladness meets the world's deep needs."[2] What Buechner calls deep gladness is that place of passion from which we best influence. Buechner gives a good rule of thumb for recognizing this place: "The kind of work God usually calls you to is the kind of work (a) that you need most to do and (b) that the world most needs to have done."[3] Influence occurs right at that intersection: at the corner where your skills, abilities, gifts, and experiences meet organization, institution, community needs. So, each day be open to opportunities that align with your passion, values, and abilities.

Look in Unexpected Places

Iris Reed is a pastor's wife, former science teacher, and former television and commercial actress. Gifted in so many ways, her

2. Buechner, *Wishful Thinking*, 119.
3. Ibid

most influential gifts now come from her platform as a small business owner. She is the owner of "Lady I ChattingBuds." A custom florist, Iris customizes floral arrangements with messages written on the flowers. She says, "For years, people have been talking to flowers and now the flowers can speak back."

Based in Chicago, Iris makes frequent trips to the flower market to get her flowers from which she makes her arrangements. At a particular intersection on this route is a building that Iris began to notice, because small groups of women convened outside the entrance. One day Iris felt compelled to look even closer and learned quite unexpectedly, the building houses a treatment center for women recovering from addictions. She shared this story:

> One day I called the center and told them that I wanted to bring flowers to the ladies. Guess what, the lady who answered the phone was named Iris. I was told that they had seven group rooms where they meet daily. So, I took them seven arrangements. They said no one has ever done anything like that for them. The reactions from the ladies were overwhelming.

When I spoke with Iris, she described the reactions when she brought the arrangements into the center. The women in treatment were surprised to know someone none of them knew was bringing something so precious just for them. The center leaders teared up noting not too many people know what they or their clients go through. You can influence people for good in what may seem like the most unexpected places.

Be Willing to State What You Want

Leona was a British business professional who was good at what she did. She learned, however, that her competence alone was not enough for her to advance into leadership if she did not use the power of her expertise to influence how others saw her. Leona was great at what she did. She was so good that her role was expanded twice, first to support leaders in her company across all of Europe, and then leaders around the globe.

Leona kept her nose to the grind, completing the necessary reports for the leaders she supported, tracking trends and other tasks assigned to her. She was competent, efficient, and focused. As good as she was, she expected her senior leaders to reward her with a promotion, not just expand her responsibilities. She saw herself as a leader, but they saw her as a technically proficient professional.

It wasn't until Leona took a course on influence that she realized it wasn't enough for her to know how good she was at her job; she had to get up out of her seat and make sure others she worked with and supported also recognized her talent and leadership potential. She committed to building her social power with the leaders she worked with, not just as a support person but also as a partner. As she tells the story, she "learned to ask for what I wanted." Her influence grew as she identified opportunities to partner with other leaders.

Like Leona, you have to be willing to state what you want. But make sure you frame and clarify how what you want benefits the collective. In the workplace, see your manager as a resource to help you clarify goals and provide assignments that are in line with organizational goals and your objectives. As you get clear on your goals, start discussing them with trusted advisors and mentors. As you see opportunities that are in line with your experiences, skill sets, and objectives, build the case for why you are a match for the opportunity. Build your confidence up and go for it.

Insert Yourself

Kerri, a leader in a professional services organization shared a story that stuck with me. Her former senior manager approached her with some things he was challenged with in the business. He said, "We're trying to figure out how to get more market share. I need some more people who understand the business. Can you help me find someone?" He noted that although Kerri was no longer in his business, she maintained excellent contacts in the business.

After their conversation, Kerri started surveying in her mind who might be a great fit for the new position. Her first inclination was to identify someone, until it dawned on her, "Hey what about me? I could take that new position and do well!"

Kerri went back to her former manager and let him know she was interested. After additional conversations, Kerri applied for and ultimately was chosen for the new role. Kerri now says that sometimes you have to insert yourself into roles or opportunities for which others may not think of you. Think about the opportunities that have your name on them and pursue them.

Take Risks

In a training program I attended recently, I had the good fortune of listening to a panel of professional coaches and business owners in which one of the women shared how she grew her business by 500 percent in four years. She made a few critical personal and professional decisions that literally changed her life. She shared with us that the key to her success was that she took some risks.

You are responsible for cultivating your influence. There will be times in which you will have to take some risks to make things happen. Don't necessarily expect others to do it for you. But by the same token, don't try to go it alone or do it by yourself. In the workplace, be willing to take stretch assignments that get the attention of management. Show that you know the business or institution and are strategic in your thinking. In your community, get out of your comfort zone to help better your corner of the world.

There are opportunities to influence all around you. Open your eyes and look to the unexpected places where your skills, abilities, gifts, and experiences can make all the difference. Someone needs just what you have to offer to make a difference in their lives. The world is waiting for you.

Put It into Action

1. Identify a woman your junior you can take to lunch or coffee and learn more about her experiences.

2. Make a list of places where your specific niche can be used to help others and better your organization or community. As you see or hear of needs, be prepared to offer solutions from your list.

Reflection/Discussion Questions

1. What hinders you from "getting out of your seat" and sharing your accomplishments with others?

2. How can tips from this chapter help move you out of your comfort zone?

10

Plan Your Path Forward

*Each of us has the right, that possibility, to invent ourselves
daily. If a person does not invent herself, she will be invented.
So, to be bodacious enough to invent ourselves is wise.*

~MAYA ANGELOU

THERE IS NO GREATER gift to ourselves than to be able to go
within ourselves and reflect on who we are and from there allow
our influence and leadership to flow. In our fast-paced world of
work and raising children, we don't often take the time for ourselves. My greatest desire for you reading this book was that you
would you take it and carve out quiet time to think, reflect, and
prepare for your greater influence. This chapter is about helping
you plan and think about the path you will take to influence for
the greater good.

Prepare

A few years ago, I was conducting an inclusive leadership pilot for
one of my New York clients. At the end of the half-day workshop,
one of the participants came up to me and asked, "Did you conduct
a women's influencing course about ten years ago in Hoboken?" I
thought for a minute and said, "Well as a matter of fact I did." She exclaimed, "I was in that workshop and that workshop was life changing. In fact, I still refer to the reference guide you supplied." *Wow!* I
thought. Over the years this woman had continued to advance, but

she attributed some of her success to a workshop that helped her explore her own power to influence. She prepared for greater influence, and from the sound of it, she continues to prepare.

Know that you will face challenges as a leader, but prepare mentally for those challenges now. You will inevitably be interrupted in a meeting. No doubt someone will try to box you into a stereotypical role. Yes, you may be made to feel like an outsider. Prepare yourself now and develop options. Prepare by learning from other women leaders who've faced similar challenges. Connect with those women leaders who speak at your women's affinity group sessions. Seek out senior women leaders to learn from.

Plan

To move forward you will need to plan for greater influence. At the end of each chapter, I provided you with tools to reflect on and put into action the principle shared in that chapter. Gather those action notes and develop a plan for yourself. As a result of this book, when it comes to the personal side of your influence what will you need to stop doing? What do you need to start doing? What do you need to continue doing?

Prioritize "I" Time

Years ago, when I worked at a large consulting firm, one of my colleagues asked, "Jeanne, what do you do to get grounded for your day?" She recognized that we were doing high-level consulting. We often worked 10-hour days and travelled about 60 percent of our time. She also knew keeping up that pace could cause any of us to frazzle and through exhaustion snap at one another or become impatient.

I'm not a perfect leader but I am a praying leader. And that's what I told her. I start my day in prayer and devotional or inspirational reading. She practiced meditation. And she began to share with me her morning ritual for preparing for her day. We both recognized the value of fueling our spirits for the work of impacting our worlds.

Never forget that you lead from who you are. Your inner world is the greatest resource for your leadership and influence. If your inner world is frazzled, disconnected, or disharmonious, then you will reflect that and even impose that on the world.

Remember Boyd Varty's recollection of Nelson Mandela. In prison Mandela went within "to think, to create within himself the things he most wanted for South Africa: peace, reconciliation, harmony." I can't help but think Mr. Mandela got a glimpse of his nation's potential for reconciliation, because he had gone through the process within himself. He could create ubuntu because he experienced it within himself.

Prioritize Self Care

We are women who wear multiple hats. We play many roles at home, at work, and in our communities; the demands of leadership are great for us. Prioritizing "I" time also means prioritizing self-care.

If you are like many of us, you don't always get that balance of self-care and other-care right. Caring for others and caring for yourself should not be mutually exclusive—but sometimes it feels that way. It seems like the nature of our work as leaders causes other-care and self-care to be polar opposites. That has to change.

We must, however, take care of ourselves and each other. We must remind ourselves of our value to this world even when the world doesn't always seem to value us. We must carve out the space to just be, to listen to the "I" within, and do the self-work, soul-work, or inner work—to care for spirit, soul, and body.

This book has been dedicated to giving you space to explore leading from within. There is a power or energy that is unleashed from leading from within your true self. You are energized by that power, and other people experience it. They feel it.

Always remember, influencing from that positive internal place can be contagious.

Put It into Action

Develop an "I" care plan that entails the following:

1. Develop a weekly schedule of reflecting on your influence goals and practices.

2. Carve out time first thing in the morning to quietly look within and envision your day.

3. Brainstorm a list of self-care activities, and then schedule them on your calendar.

Reflection/Discussion Questions

1. As a result of completing this book, what is your next step?

2. What are the things you've been doing up to this point that you now need to stop in order to strengthen your influence?

3. What are the things you've been doing up to this point that you now need to start doing to strengthen your influence?

4. What are the things you've been doing as a leader up to this point that you need to continue?

Acknowledgments

It takes a village to write a book, and I am so grateful for my village.

I must acknowledge my circle of sister friends who support each other in every endeavor. You know who you are, and you show up in this book on the pages but also in the heart of the author.

A special thanks to Dr. Valerie Landfair for giving the draft manuscript a very close read. Your ideas strengthened this book. Thank you, Dr. Phillis Sheppard, for connecting me with Wipf and Stock Publishers. Thank you, Jennifer LuVert, for providing both developmental and copyediting. I always enjoy working with you. Thank you, Matt Wimer, for accepting this book into the Resource imprint.

As I was finishing this book, I completed a coaching certification training program led by Mina Brown, Peggy Dean, and Meg Rentschler of the Coach Academy International. Thank you for presenting models that enabled me to more clearly think through the frameworks presented in this book.

Finally, to the many women across the globe who have participated in my women's training sessions for the past fifteen or so years: thank you for your insights and openness that made the lessons in this book possible.

Bibliography

Banaji, Mahzarin R., and Anthony Greenwald. *Blindspot: Hidden Biases of Good People*. New York: Delacorte, 2013.

Barash, Susan Shapiro. *Tripping the Prom Queen: The Truth About Women and Rivalry*. New York: St Martin's, 2006.

Buechner, Frederick. *Wishful Thinking: A Seeker's ABC*. San Francisco: Harper SanFrancisco, 1993.

Cashman, Kevin. *Leadership from the Inside Out: Becoming a Leader for Life*. San Francisco: Berrett-Koehler, 2008.

Catalyst. "Women 'Take Care' and Men 'Take Charge:' Stereotypes of U.S. Business Leaders Exposed." New York: Catalyst, 2005. https://www.catalyst. org/knowledge/women-take-care-men-take-charge-stereotyping-us-business-leaders-exposed

Eilperin, Juliet. "White House Women Want to Be in the Room Where It Happens." Washington Post, September 13, 2016. https://www.washingtonpost.com/news/powerpost/wp/2016/09/13/white-house-women-are-now-in-the-room-where-it-happens/?noredirect=on&utm_term=.637adae54350

French, J. R. P., Jr., and B. Raven. "The Bases of Social Power." In Dorwin P. Cartwright (Ed.), *Studies in Social Power* (150–167). Ann Arbor, Michigan: Institute for Social Research, University of Michigan, 1959, 159–167.

Follett, Mary Parker. *Prophet of Management: A Celebration of Writings from the 1920s*. Pauline Graham (ed.), Washington DC: Beard Books, 2003.

Gerzema, John, and Michael D'Antonio. *The Athena Doctrine: How Women (and the Men Who Think Like them) Will Rule the Future*. San Francisco: Jossey-Bass, 2013.

Gladwell, Malcolm. *The Tipping Point: How Little Things Can Make a Big Difference*. New York: Little Brown and Company, 2002.

Harris, Aisha. "She Founded Me Too, Now She wants to Move Past the Trauma." *The New York Times*, October 15, 2018. https://www.nytimes.com/2018/10/15/arts/tarana-burke-metoo-anniversary.html?emc=edit_th_181016&nl=todaysheadlines&nlid=450988191016

Harris, Carla. *Expect to Win: 10 Proven Strategies for Thriving in the Workplace*. New York: Hudson Street, 2009.

Ibarra, Herminia, Robin Ely, and Deborah Kolb. "Women Rising: The Unseen Barriers." *Harvard Business Review*, September 2013.

Ibarra, Herminia. "Building Effective Networks." Stanford Michelle R. Clayman Institute for Gender Research. n.d. https://womensleadership.stanford.edu/ building-effective-networks

Kanter, Rosabeth Moss. *Confidence: How Winning and Losing Streaks Begin and End.* New York: Crown Publishing, 2012.

Kay, Katty, and Claire Shipman. *The Confidence Code: The Science and Art of Self-Assurance—What Women Should Know.* New York: Harper Collins, 2014.

Keltner, Dacher. *The Power Paradox: How We Gain and Lose Influence.* New York: Penguin Books, 2016.

Lais, Becca. "The Purposeful Silencing of Black Women In Educational Leadership." *The Black Wall Street Times*, February 8, 2018. https://theblack wallsttimes.com/2018/02/08/the-purposeful-silencing-of-black-women-in-educational-leadership/

Lerner, Helene. *The Confidence Myth: Why Women Undervalue Their Skills and How to Get Over It!* San Francisco: Berrett Koehler, 2015.

Magliozzi, Devon. *Building Effective Networks: Nurturing Strategic Relationships, Especially for Women.* Stanford The Clayman Institute for Gender Research, April 26, 2016. https://gender.stanford.edu/news-publications/ gender-news/building-effective-networknurturing-strategic-relationships

Matshe, Gertrude. *Born on the Continent: Ubuntu.* Wellington, New Zealand: Gertrude Matshe, 2012.

May, Kate Torgovnick. "I Am, Because of You: Further Reading on Ubuntu." Ted talks Blog. https://blog.ted.com/further-reading-on-ubuntu/

Obama, Michelle. *Becoming.* New York: Crown, 2018.

Palmer, Parker. *Let Your Life Speak: Listening for the Voice of Vocation.* San Francisco: Jossey-Bass, 2000.

P&G. *Pantene Philippines #WhipIt Campaign Goes Global Virally.* P&G Press Release, 2012.

PWC. Mending the Gender Gap, 2013.

Robb, Carly. "Ubuntu: I Am Because You Are." *Medium*, March 14, 2017. https:// medium.com/thrive-global/ubuntu-i-am-because-you-are-66efa03f2682

Santiago, Cassandra and Doug Criss. "An Activist, a Little Girl and the Heartbreaking Origin of 'Me Too.'" CNN, October 17, 2017. https://www. cnn.com/2017/10/17/us/me-too-tarana-burke-origin-trnd/index.html

Starecheski, Laura. Why Saying Is Believing — The Science of Self-Talk; https:// www.npr.org/sections/health-shots/2014/10/07/353292408/why-saying-is-believing-the-science-of-self-talk

Tutu, Desmond. *God Has a Dream: A Vision of Hope for Our Time.* New York: Doubleday, 2004.

CPSIA information can be obtained
at www.ICGtesting.com
Printed in the USA
FSHW020706170419

9 781532 662942